Y0-BGV-477

Design
and
Compilations
by
D'Bee

Copyright TXu 1-845-825
All content in this book (including compilations and punctuation, in their unique sequencing and combination with images, any improvements or modifications to such content; and any derivative works) is the property of ©2012, D'Bee LLC. All rights reserved. Including the right of reproduction or transmission in whole or in part in any form. Images are protected under the U.S. copyright.

All quotations remain the intellectual property of their respective originators. And there is no claim of copyright for individual quotations. All use of quotations is done under the fair use copyright principle.

Sources
Bartleby.com, brainyquote.com, famousquotes.com, famousquotesandauthors.com, goodquotes.com, goodreads.com, notable-quotes.com, quotationspage.com, quotationsbook.com, quote-museum.com, quotesdaddy.com, searchquotes.com, thinkexist.com, wikiquote.org, Google Books, *A Cyclopaedia of nature teachings* (1892), *The Oxford Dictionary of Quotations*.

A portion of the proceeds from this book is allocated to charity.

For Donna, Kay, Bruce, Dawn, Bobby, Daniel, Pat, Cindy, Greg, Jane, Steve, Maria, John, Susan, Mariam, Meg, Bob, and Riley…

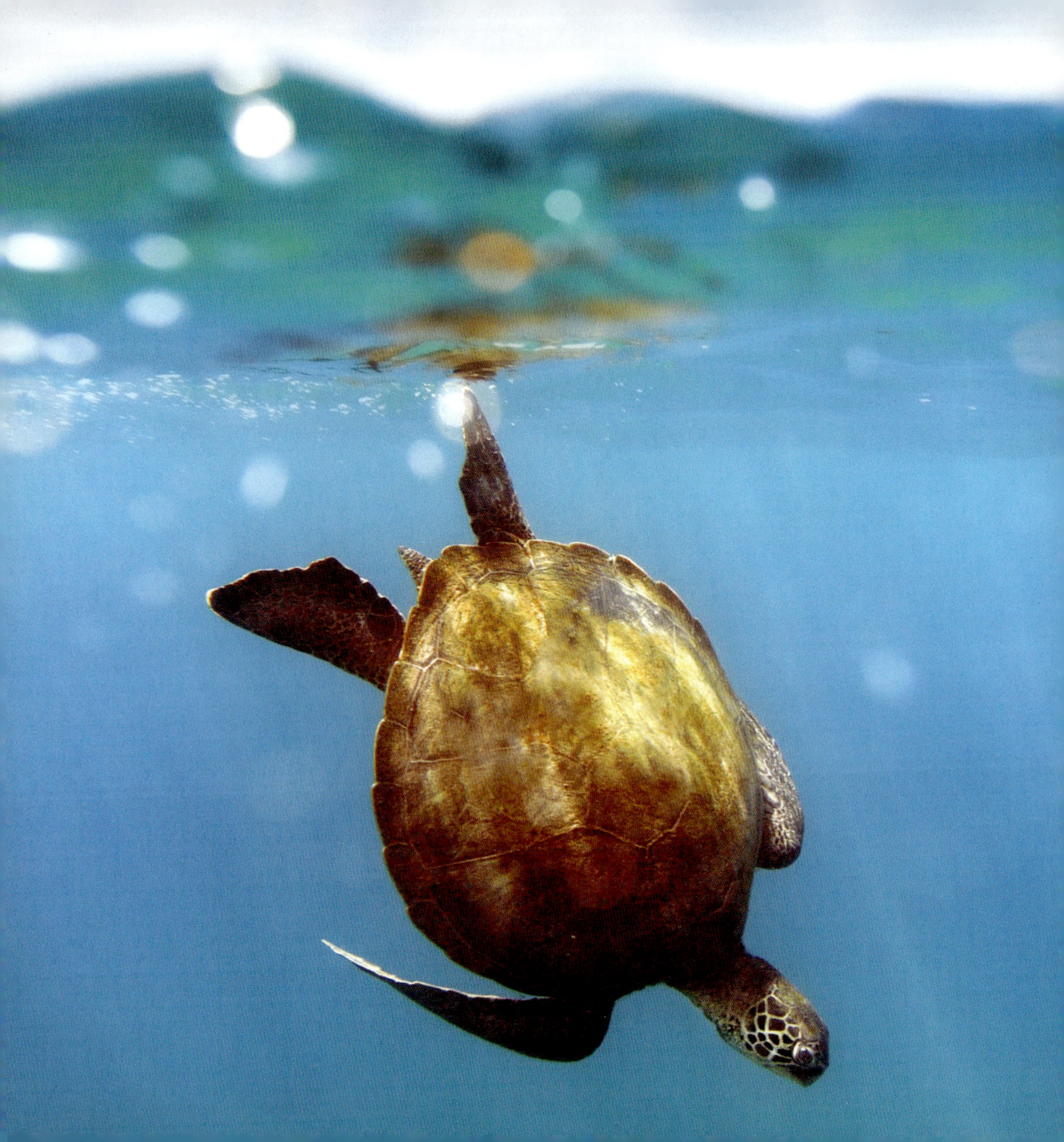

You cannot discover

new oceans

unless you have

the courage

to lose sight of

the shore.

André Gide

Why do we love the sea?
It is because
it has some potent power
to make us think
things we like to think.

Robert Henri

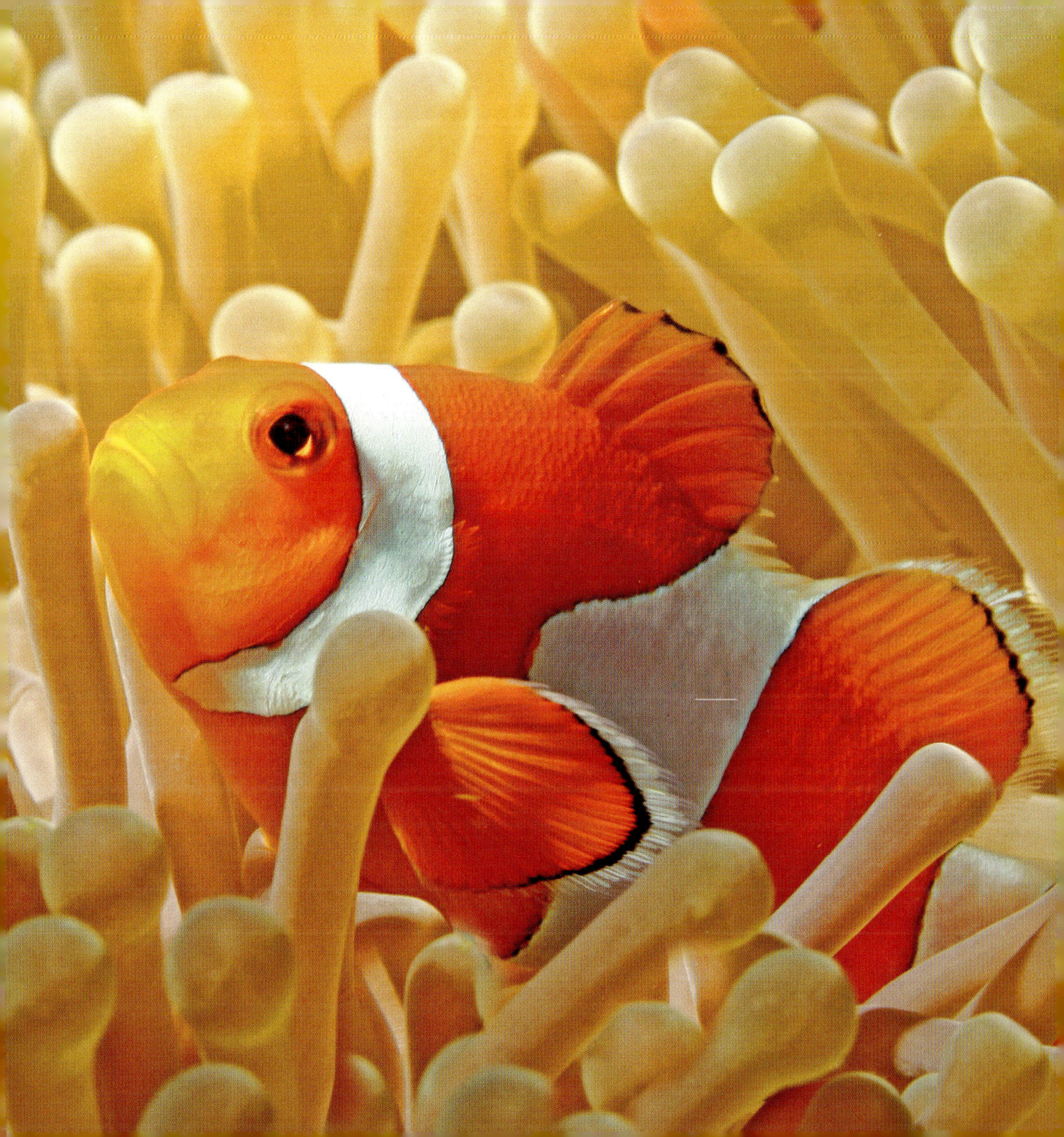

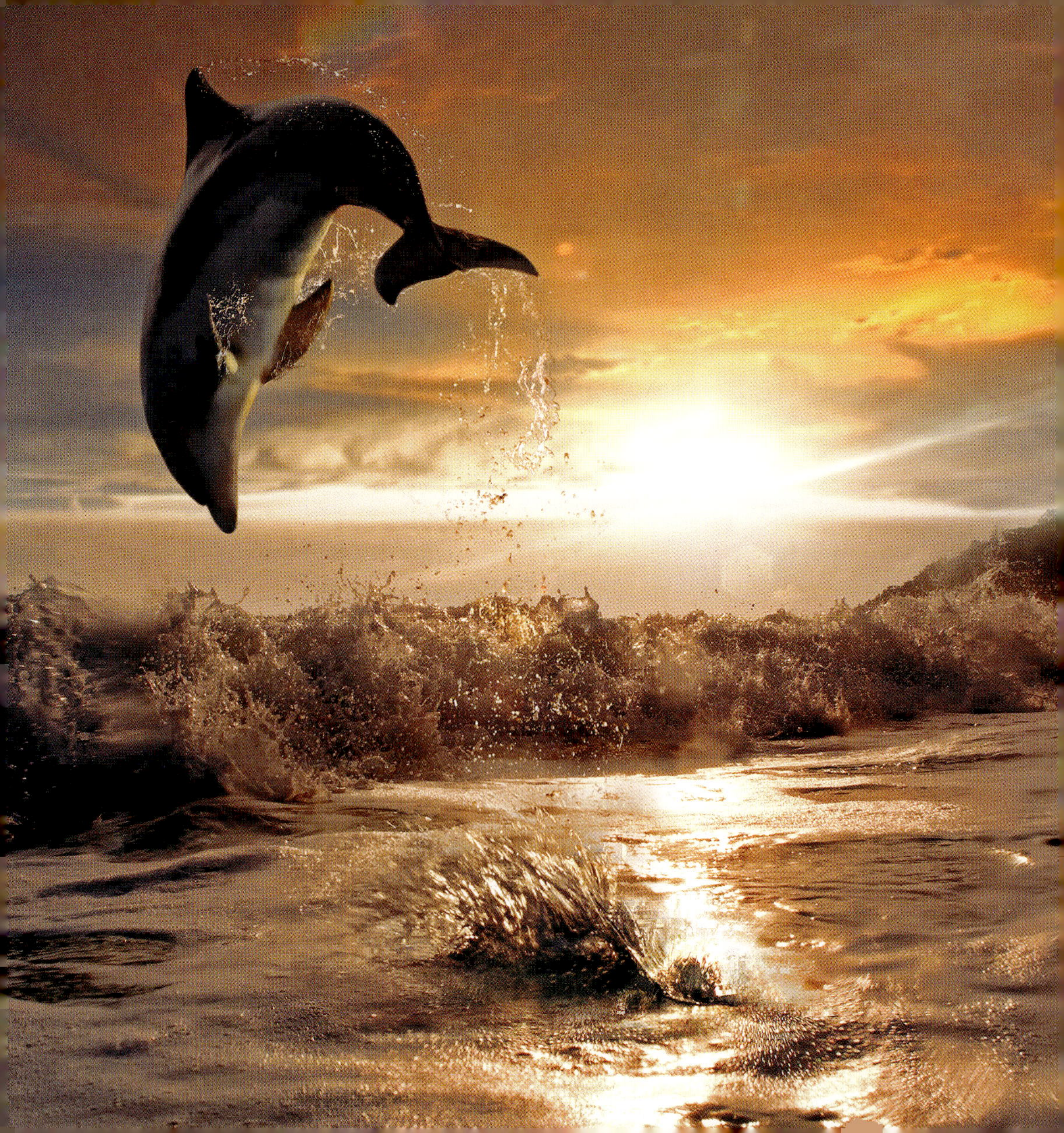

Weak minds

sink under prosperity

as well as adversity;

but strong and deep ones

have two high tides.

Alexander Smith

I've never

let my school

interfere

with my education.

Mark Twain

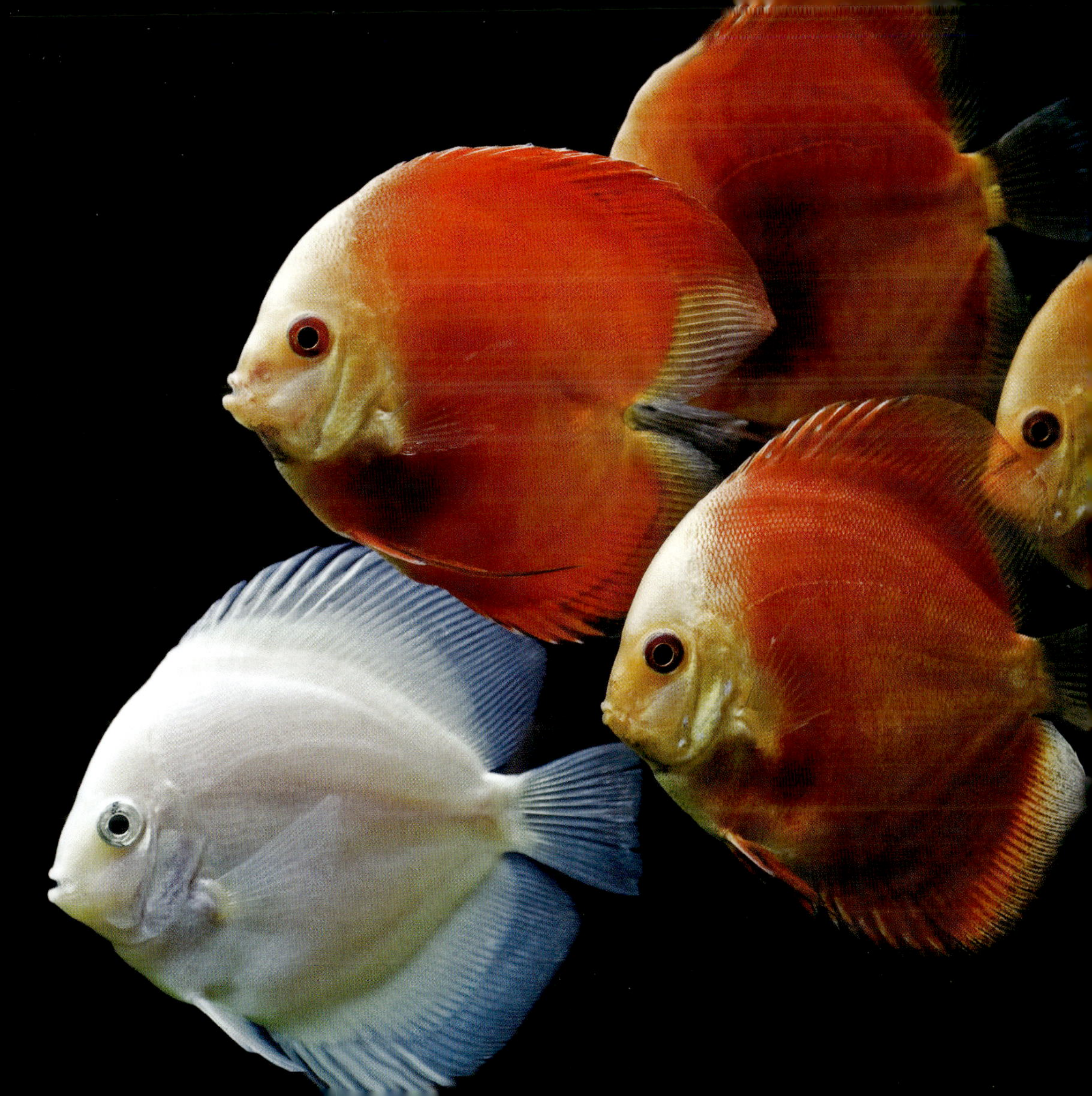

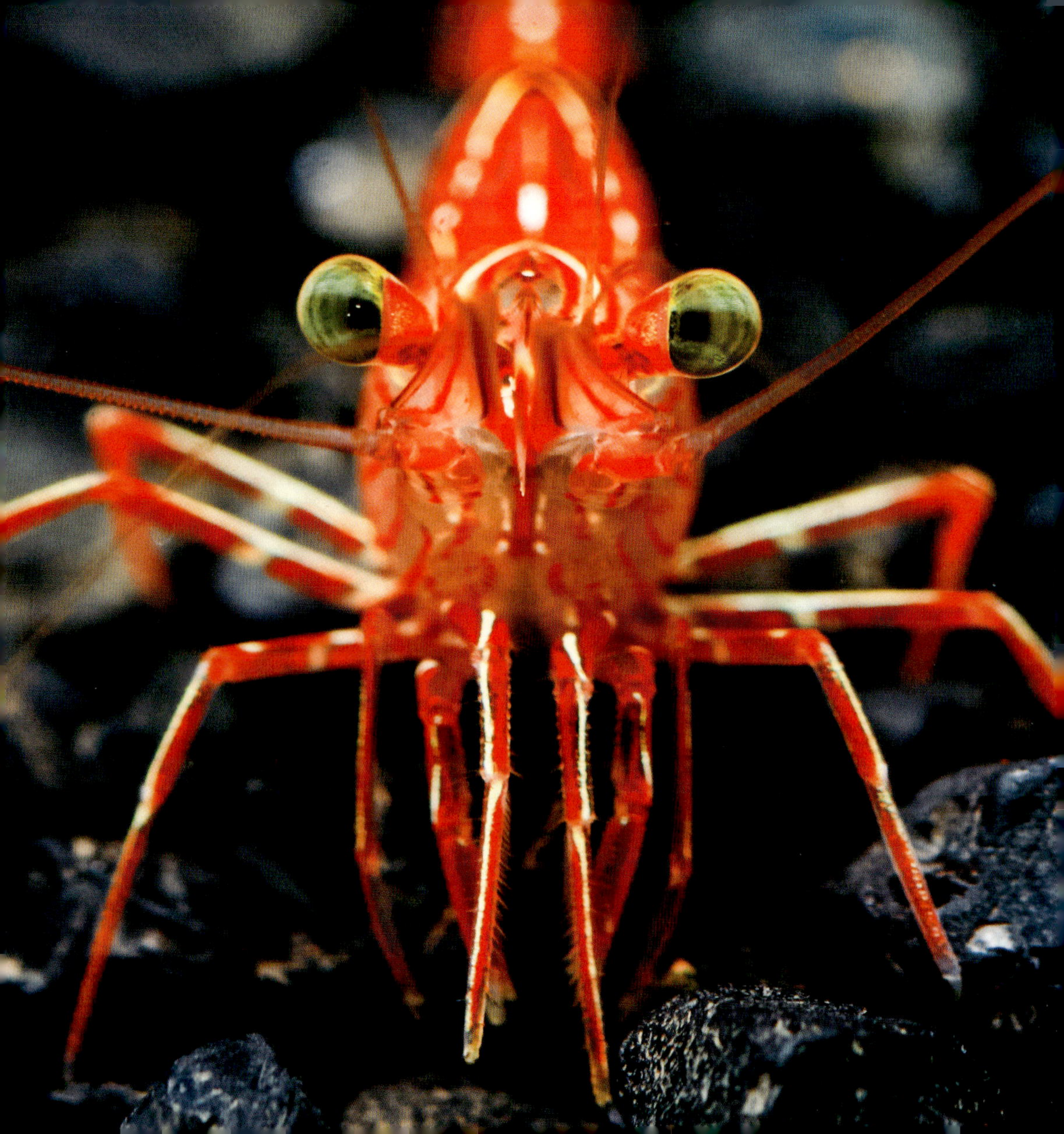

I see too deep and too much.

Henri Barbusse

Originality is simply a pair of fresh eyes.

Thomas W. Higginson

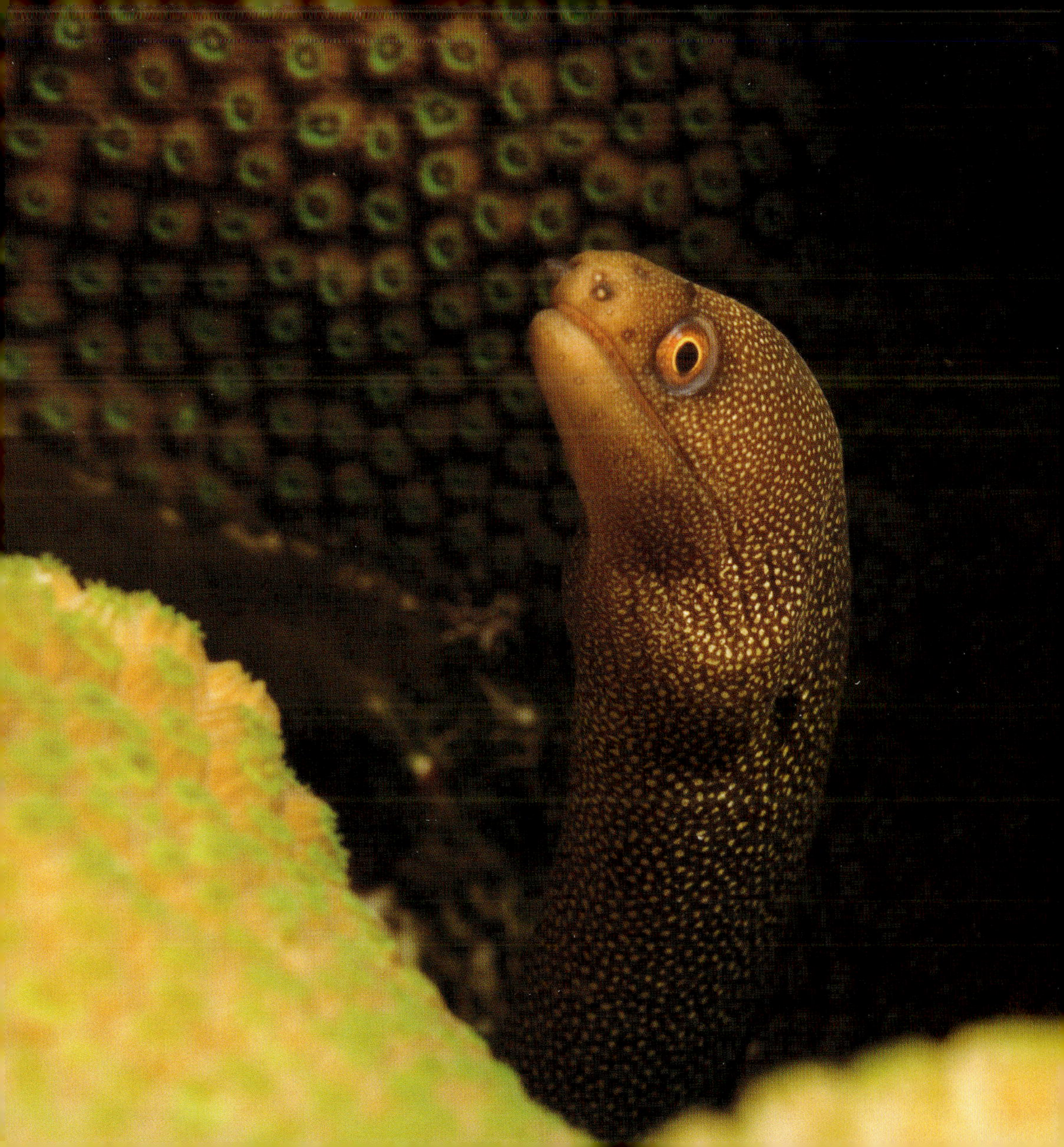

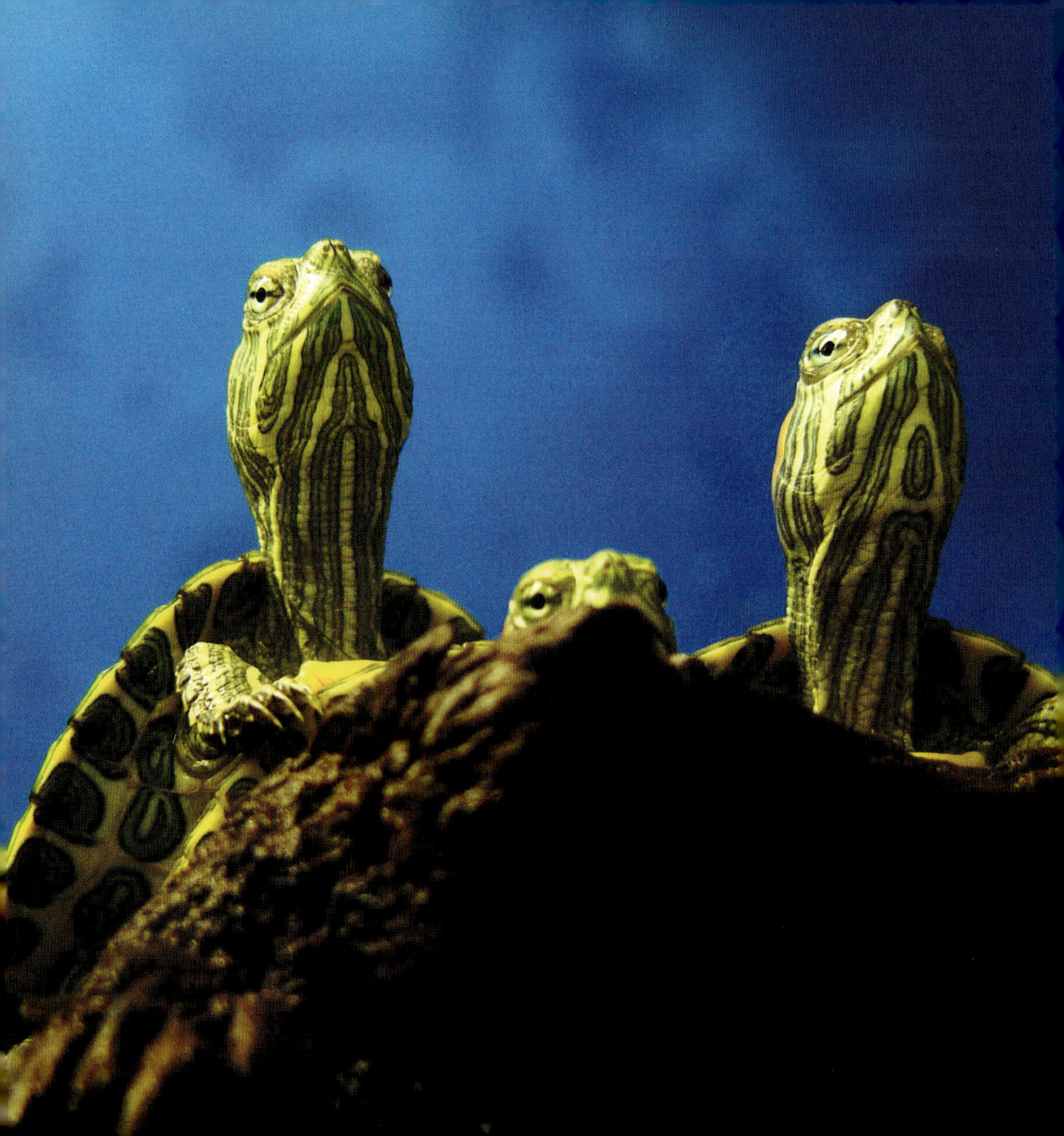

You can't cross the sea

merely by standing

and staring at the water.

Rabindranath Tagore

The least movement

is of importance to all nature.

The entire ocean

is affected by a pebble.

Blaise Pascal

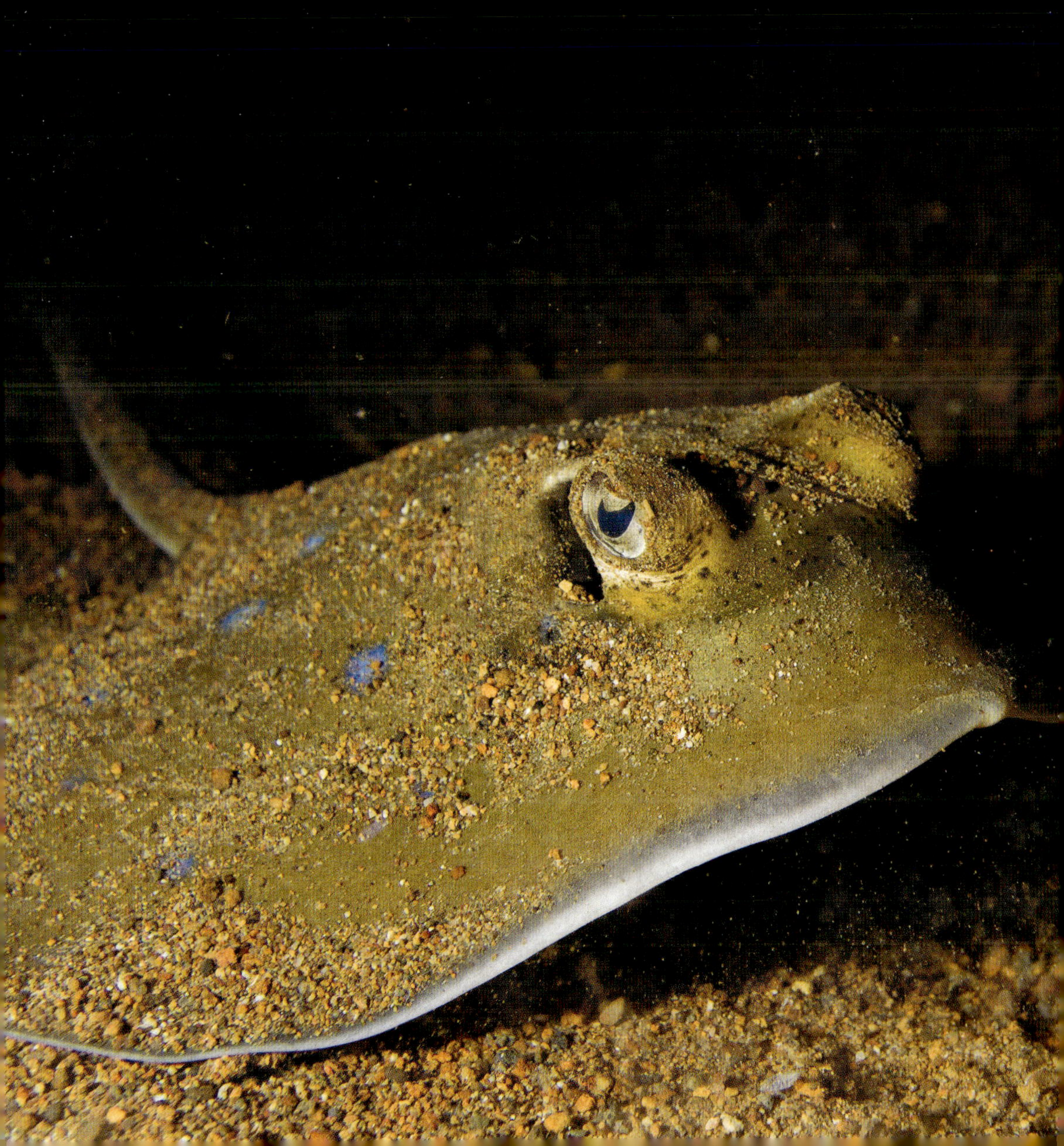

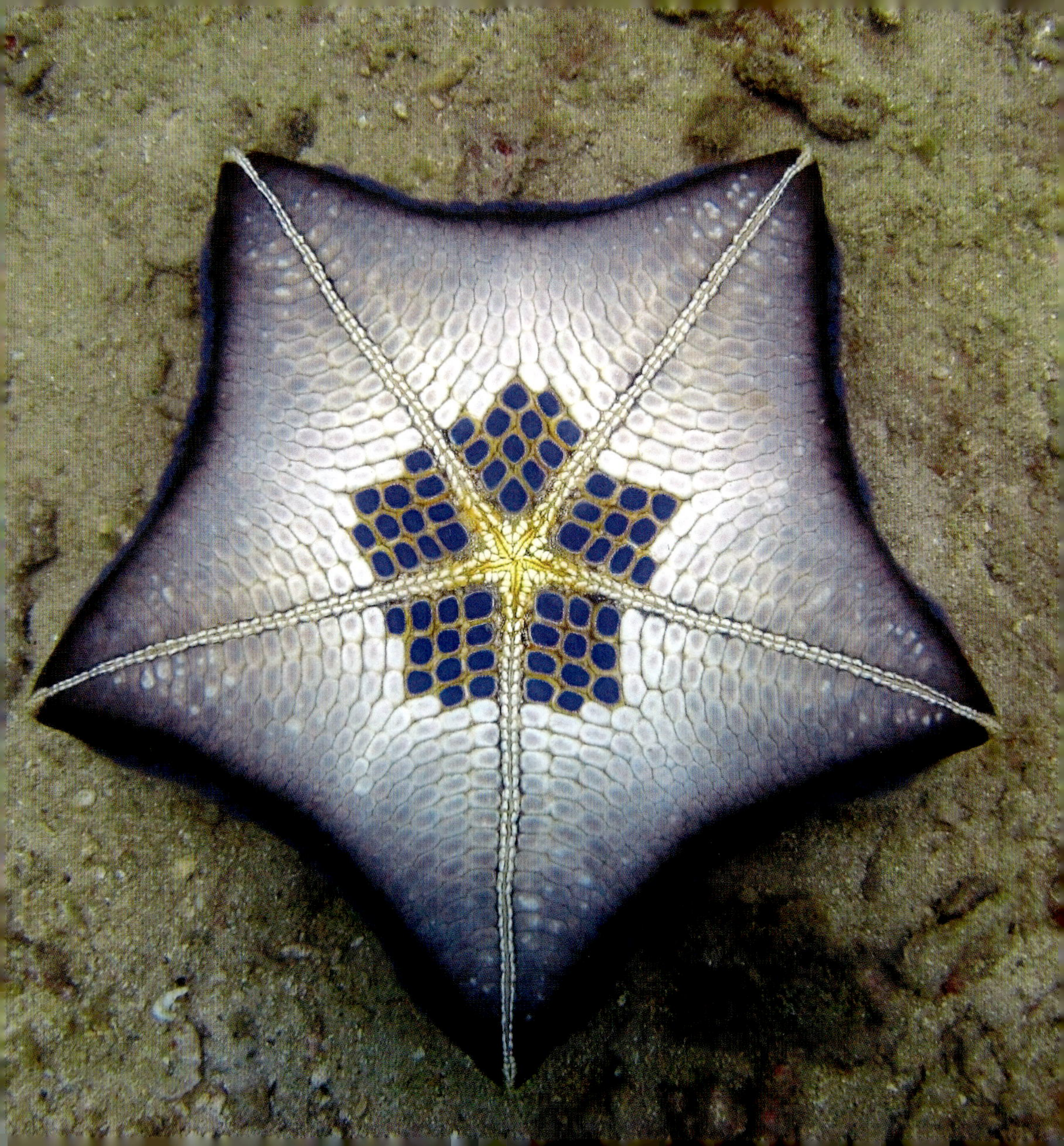

In one drop of water

are found all the secrets of the oceans.

Khalil Gibran

When one tugs
at a single thing in nature
he finds it attached
to the rest of the world.

John Muir

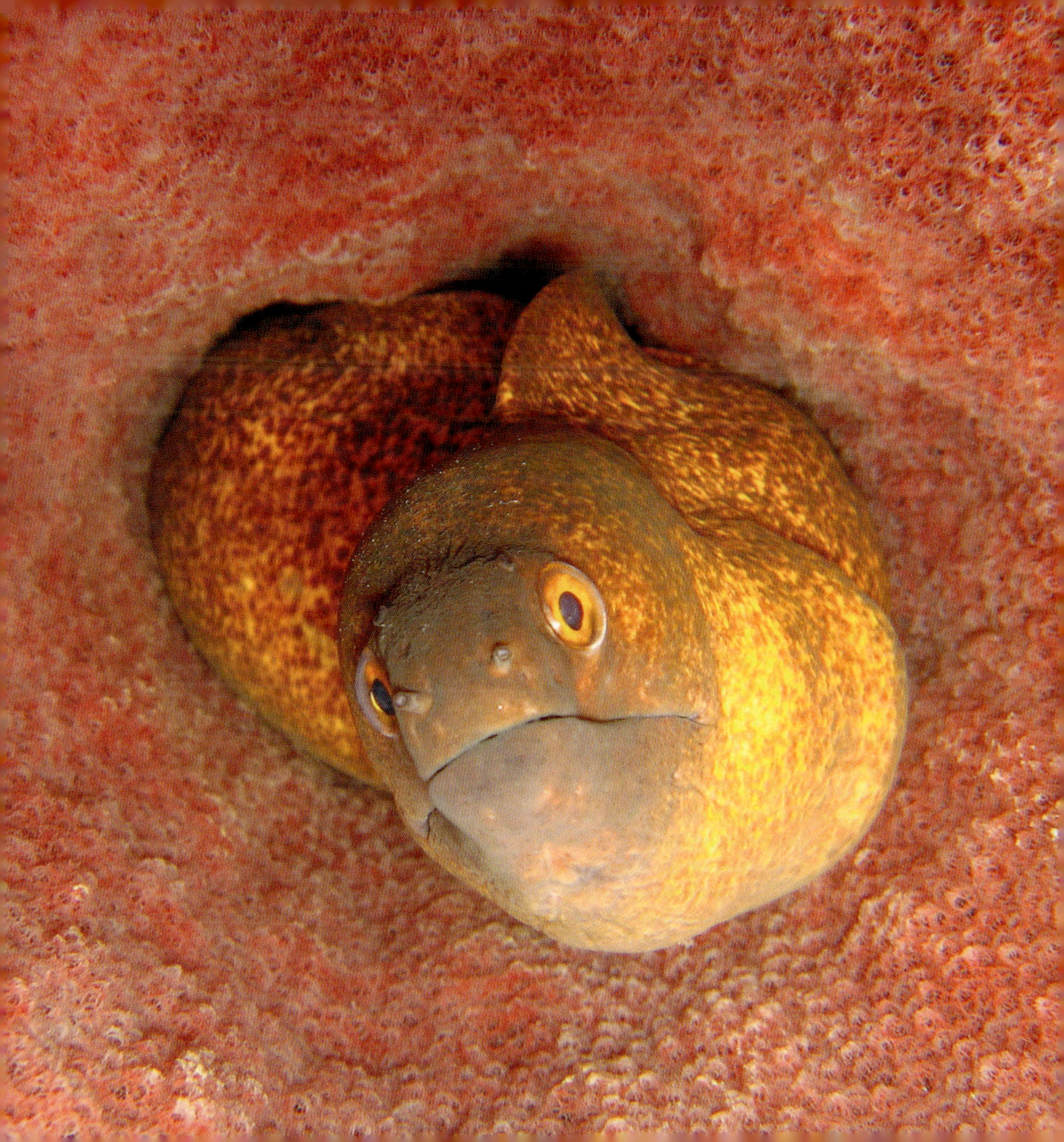

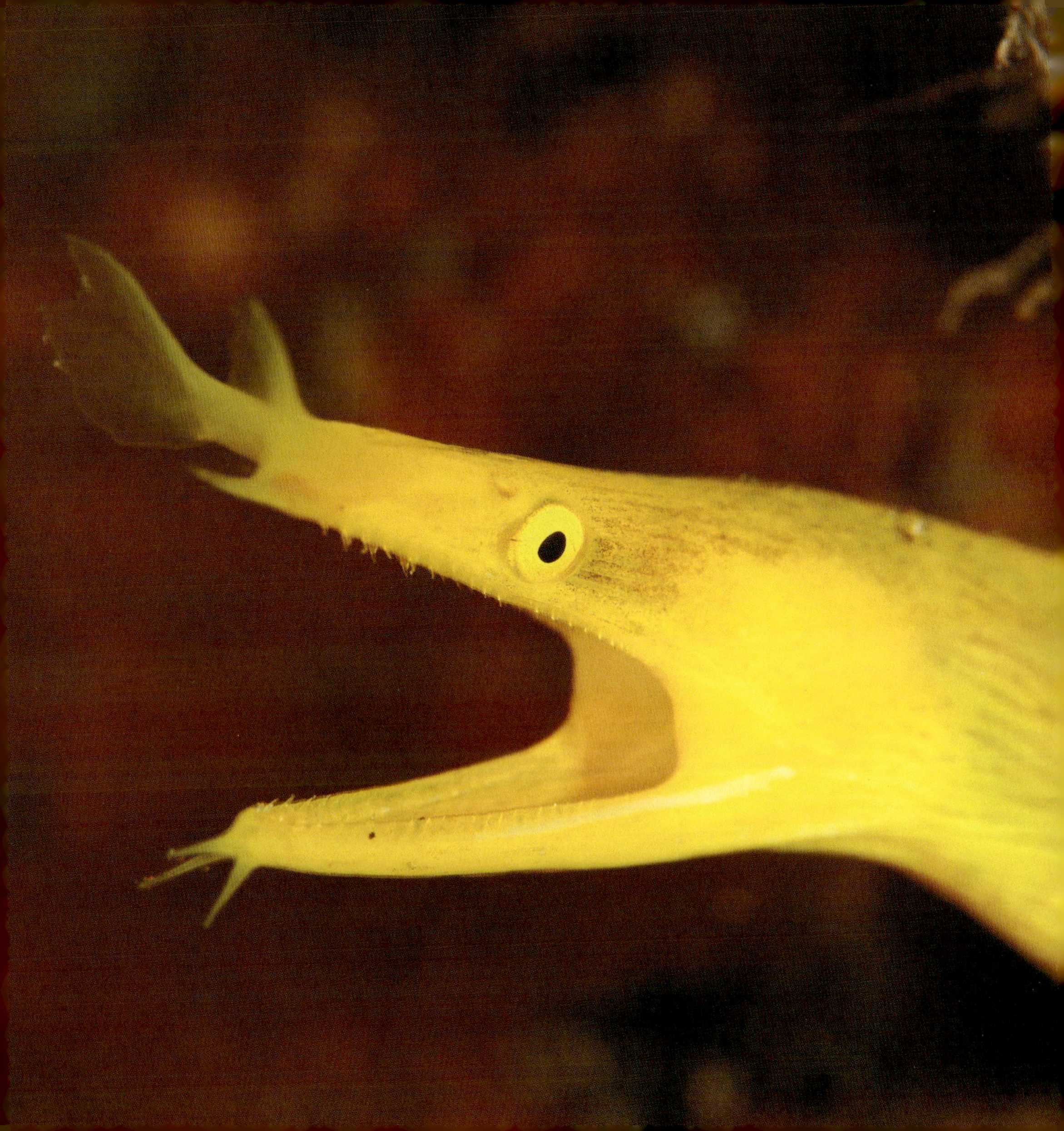

But doth suffer a sea-change

Into something rich and strange

William Shakespeare

Deep experience is never peaceful.

Henry James

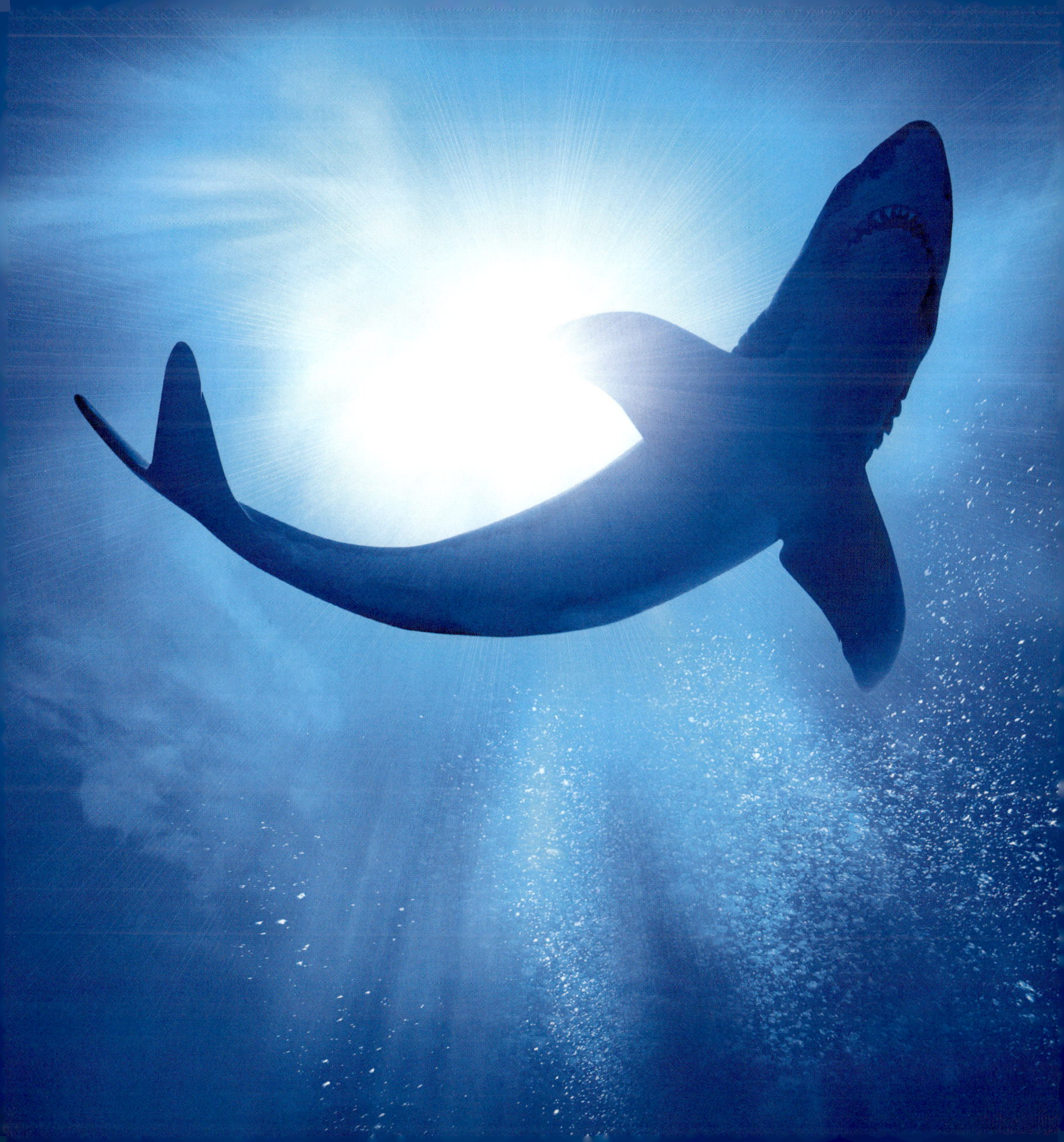

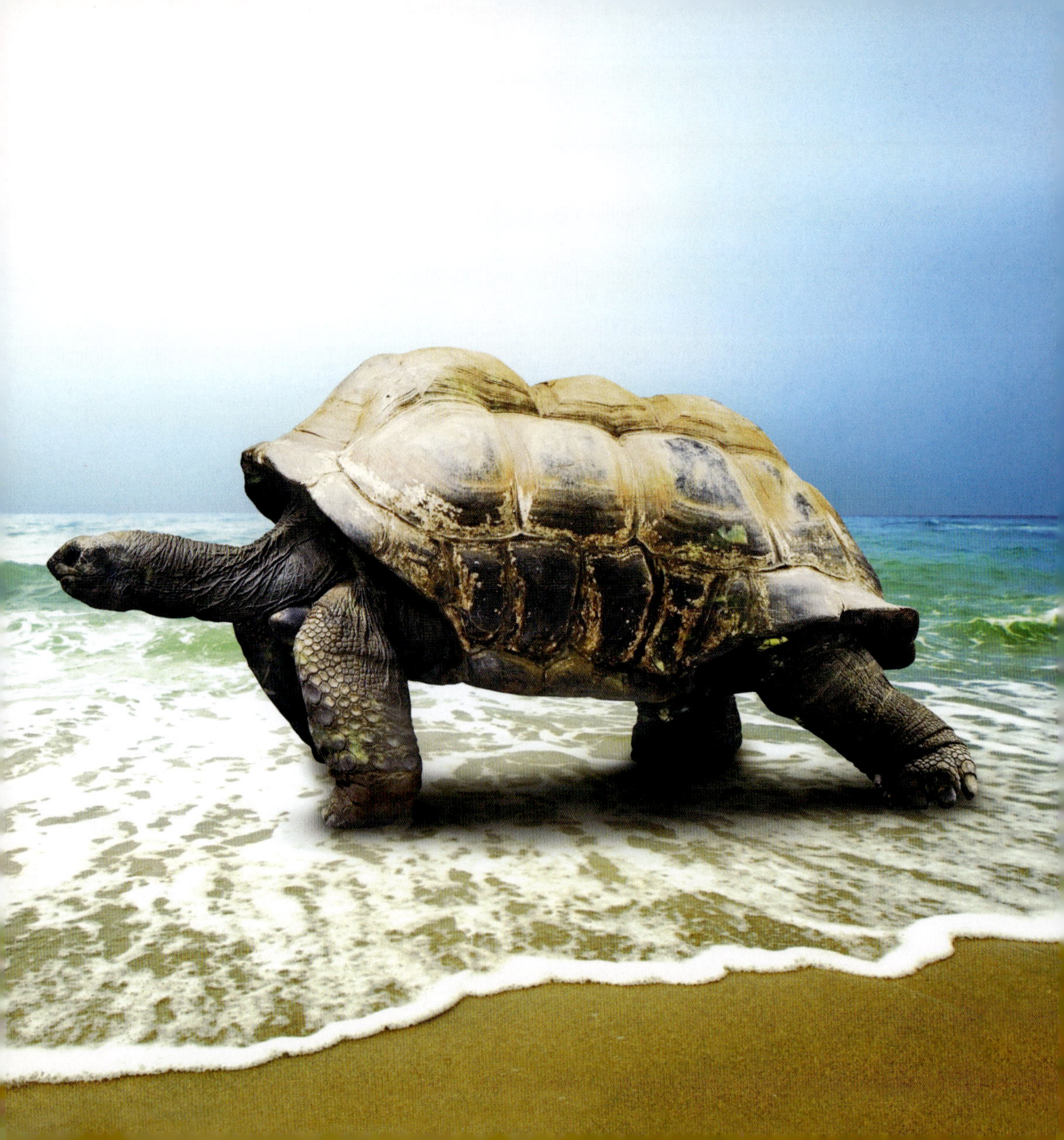

When I was a youth the Dead Sea was only sick.

George Burns

It is not length of life,
but depth of life.

Ralph Waldo Emerson

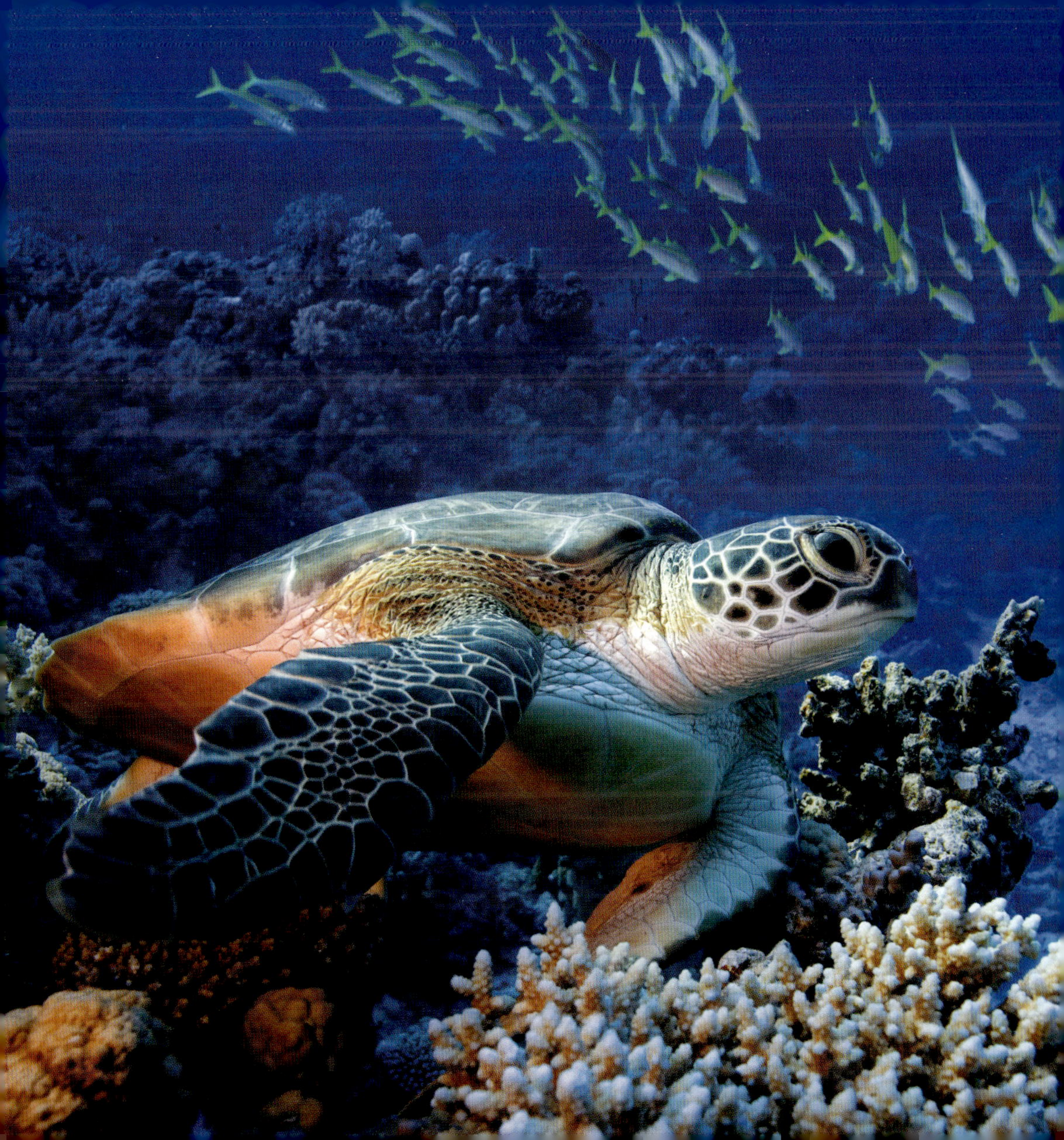

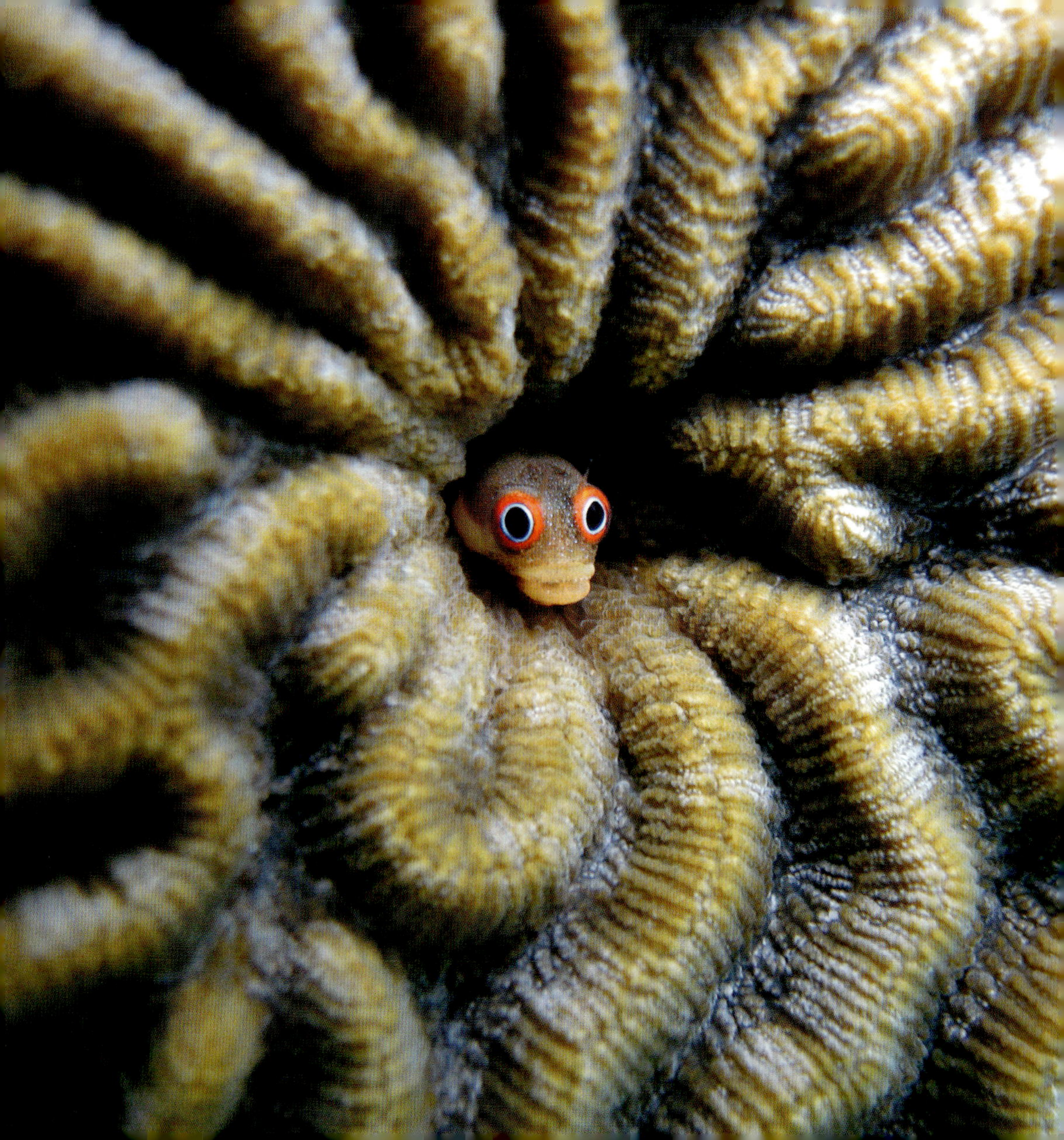

Don't
fight forces,
use them.

Buckminster Fuller

Remember,
a dead fish can float
downstream,
but it takes
a live one to swim
upstream.

W. C. Fields

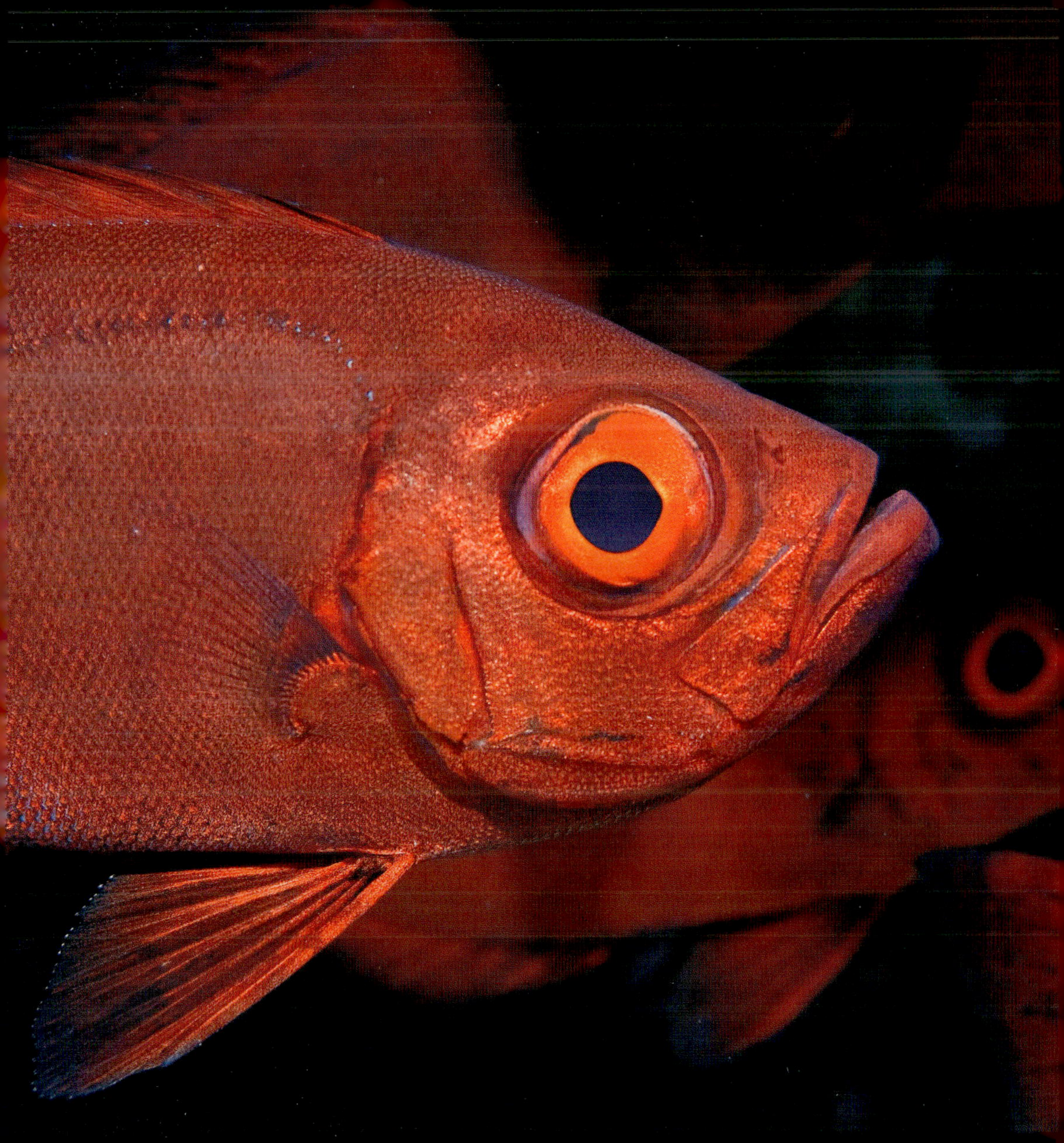

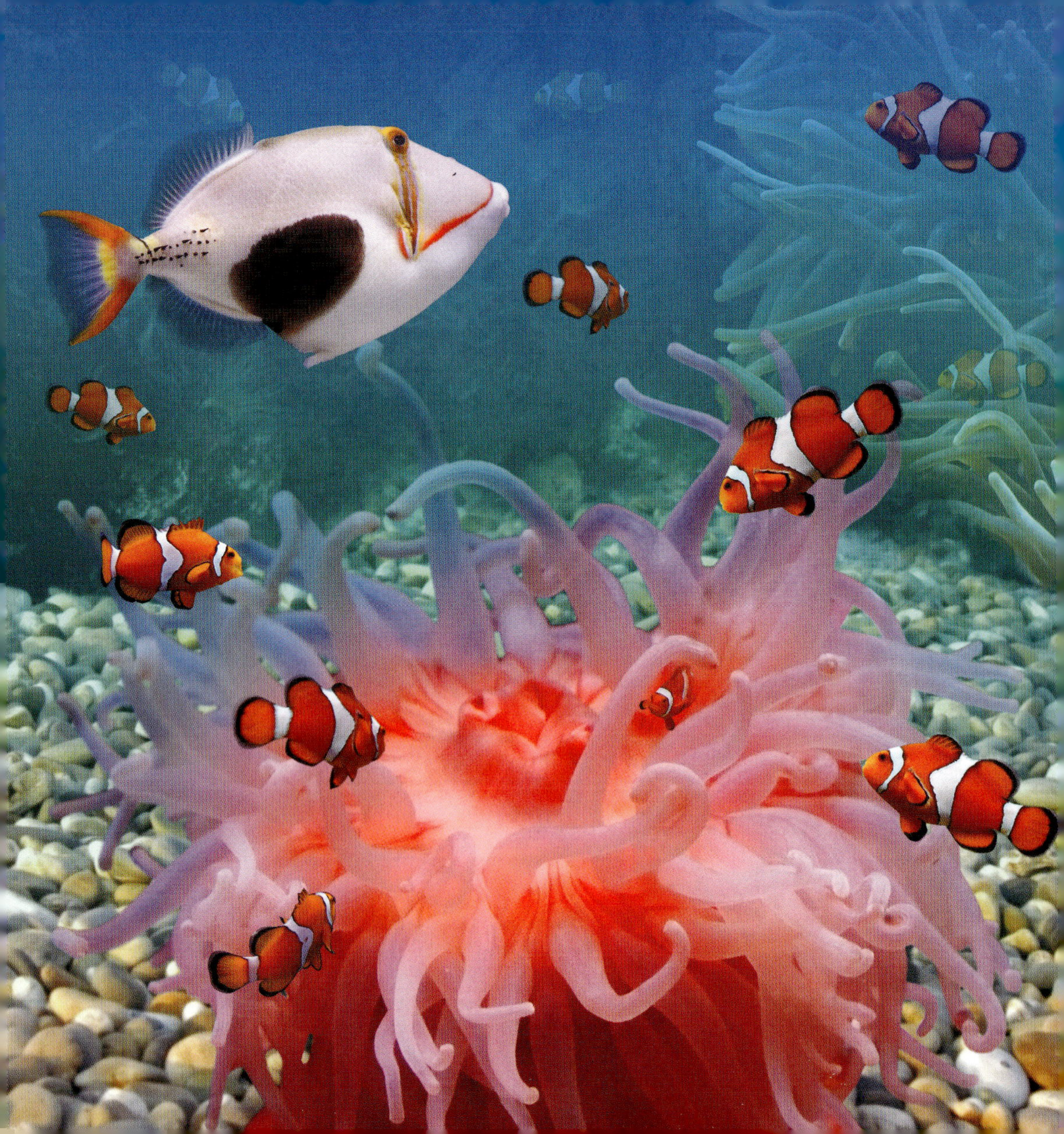

The ocean is a mighty harmonist.

William Wordsworth

Look at that sea...

all silver and shadow

and vision of things not seen.

We couldn't enjoy

its loveliness any more

if we had millions of dollars

and ropes of diamonds.

L.M. Montgomery

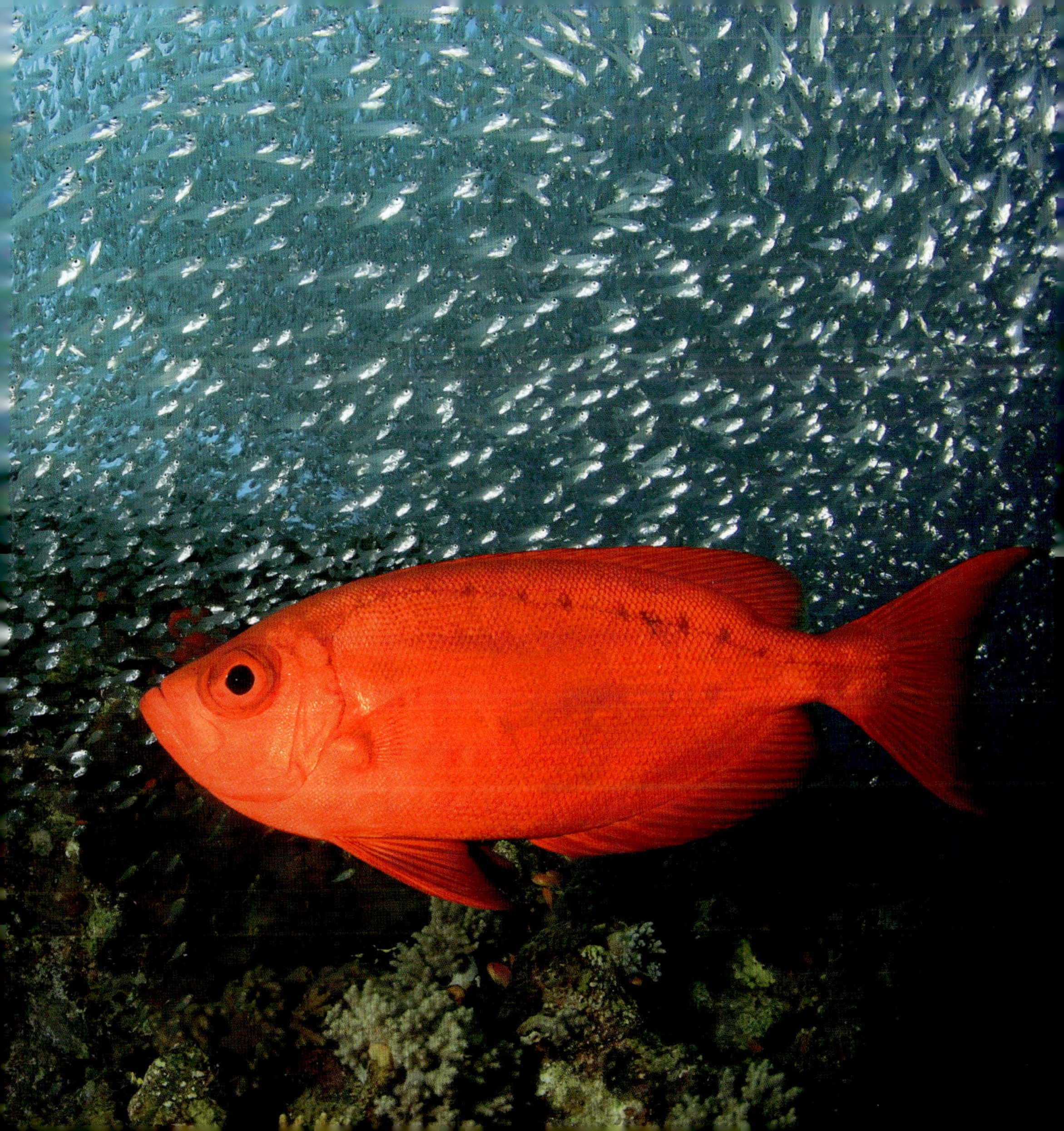

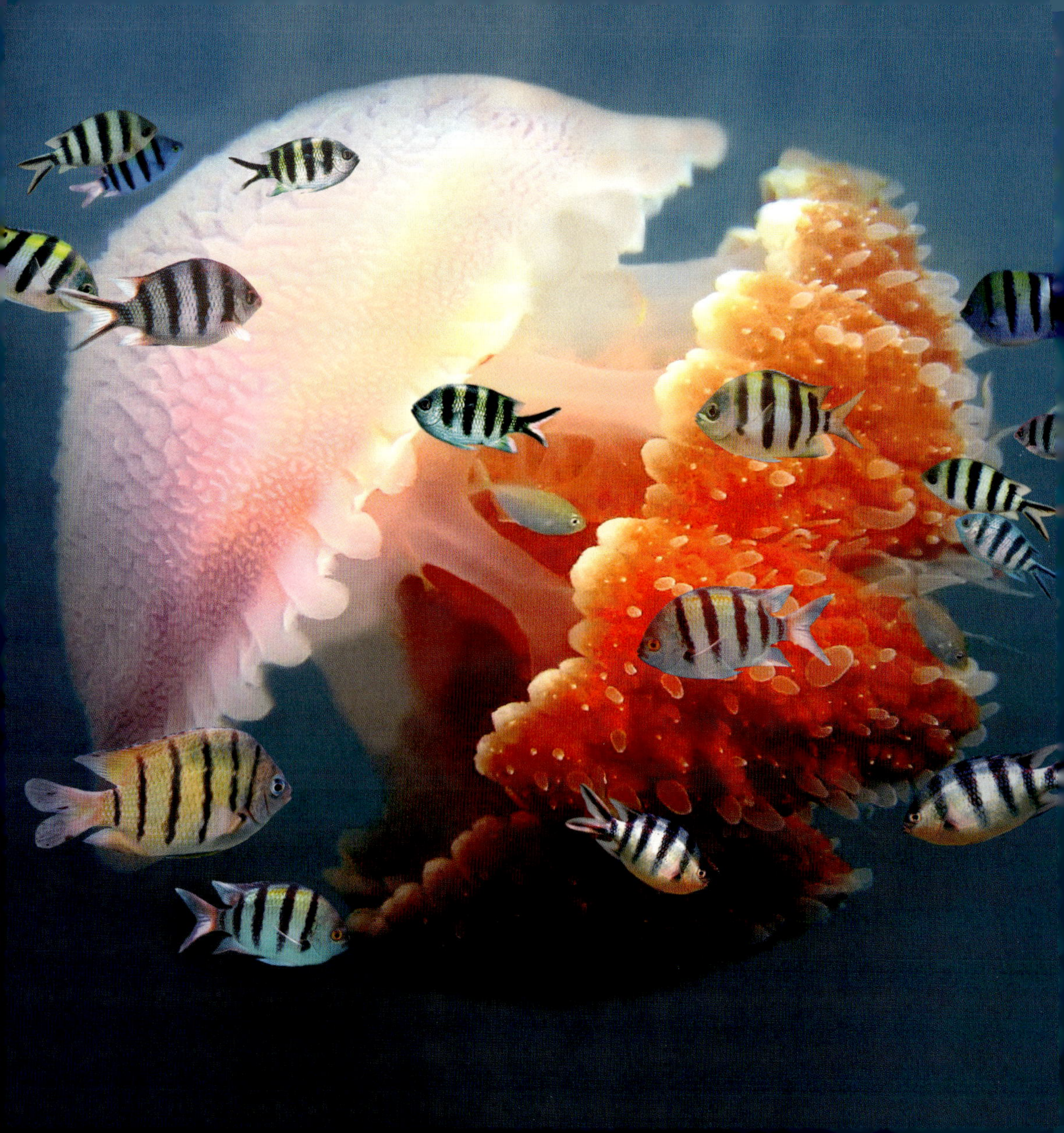

We forget

that the water cycle

and the

life cycle are one.

Jacques-Yves Cousteau

All the rivers run into the sea;

yet the sea is not full.

King Solomon

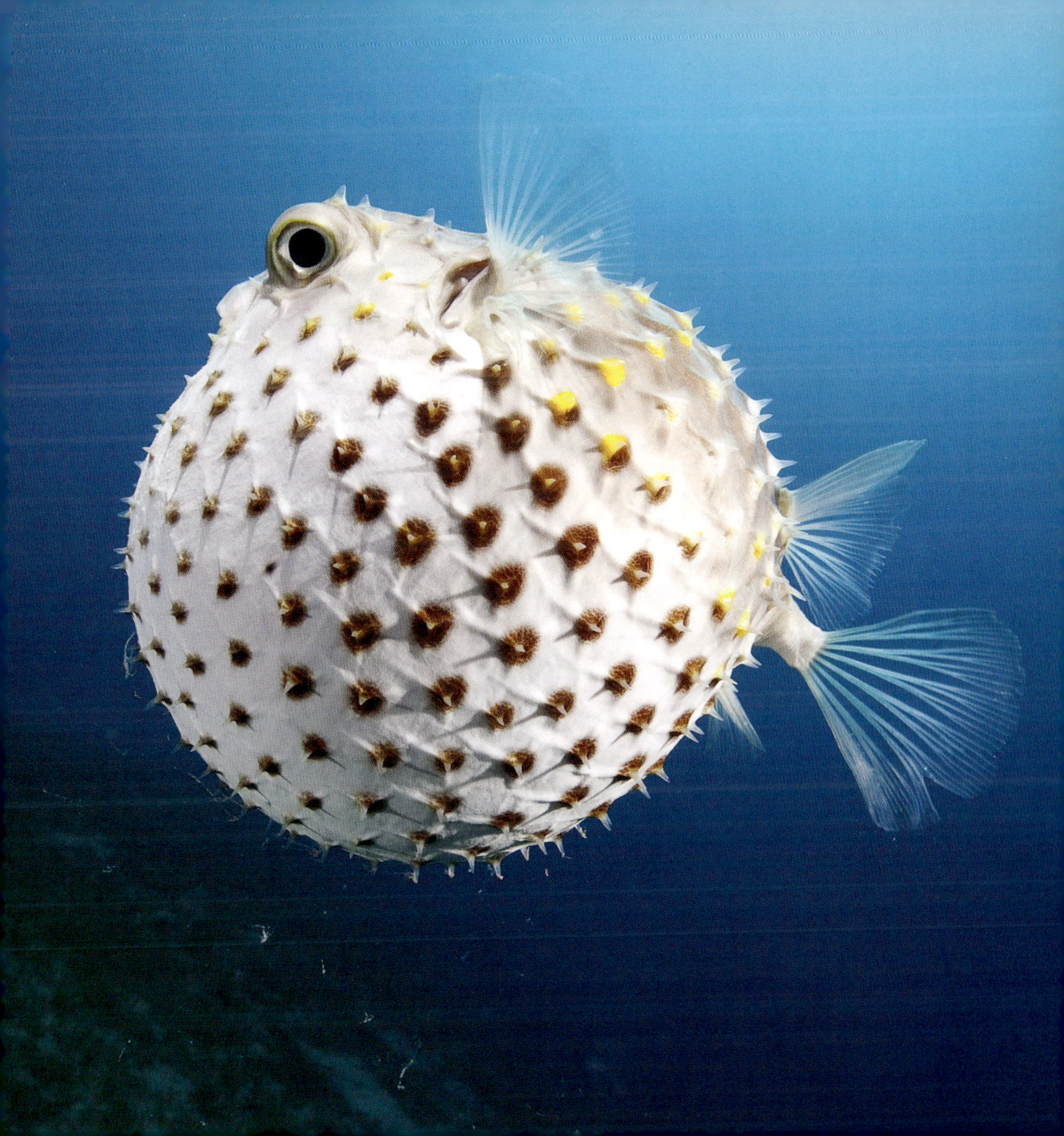

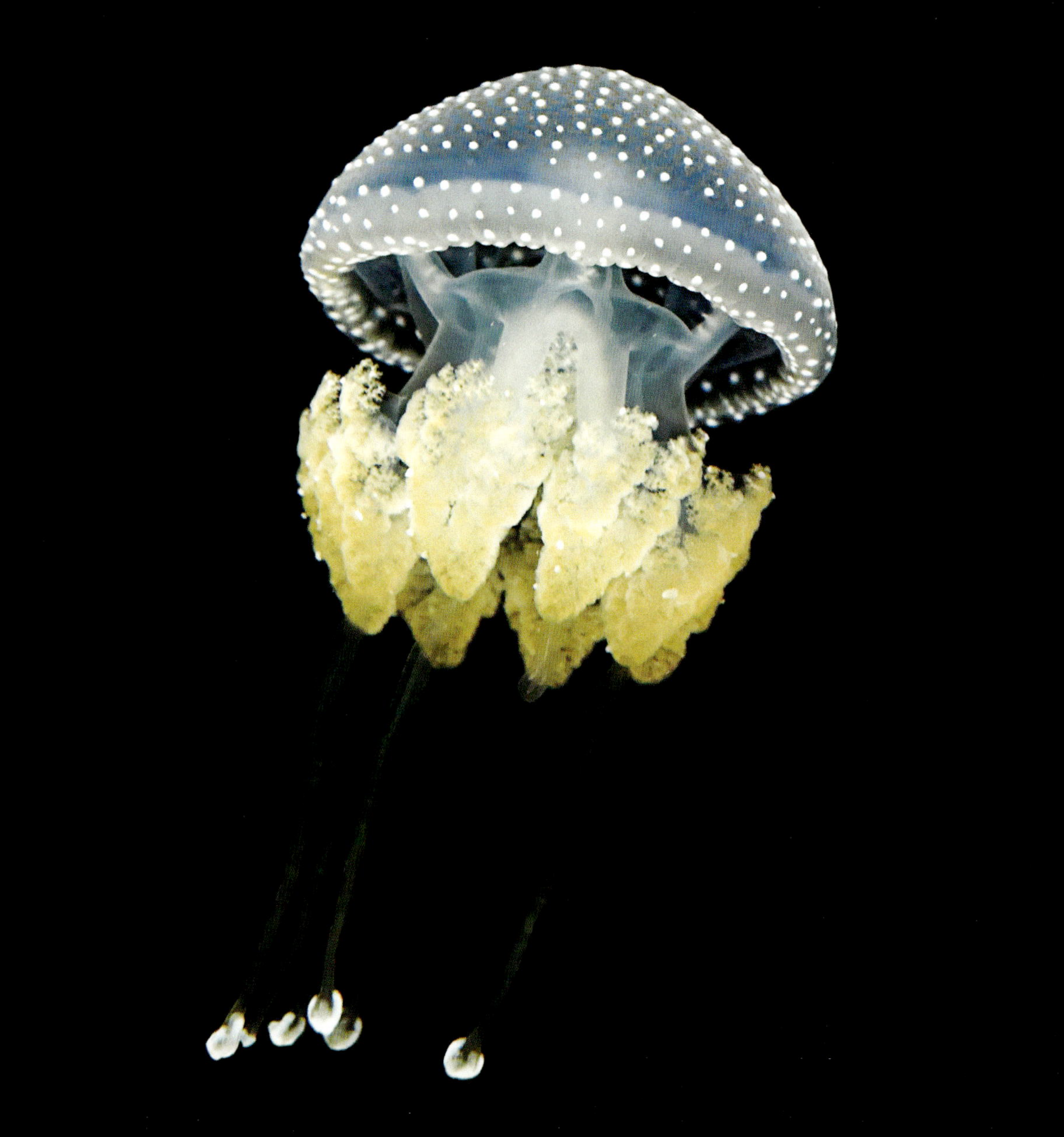

There is

one spectacle grander

than the sea,

that is the sky;

there is

one spectacle grander

than the sky,

that is the interior

of the soul.

Victor Hugo

The voice of the sea speaks

to the soul.

The touch of the sea

is sensuous,

enfolding the body

in its soft,

close embrace.

Kate Chopin

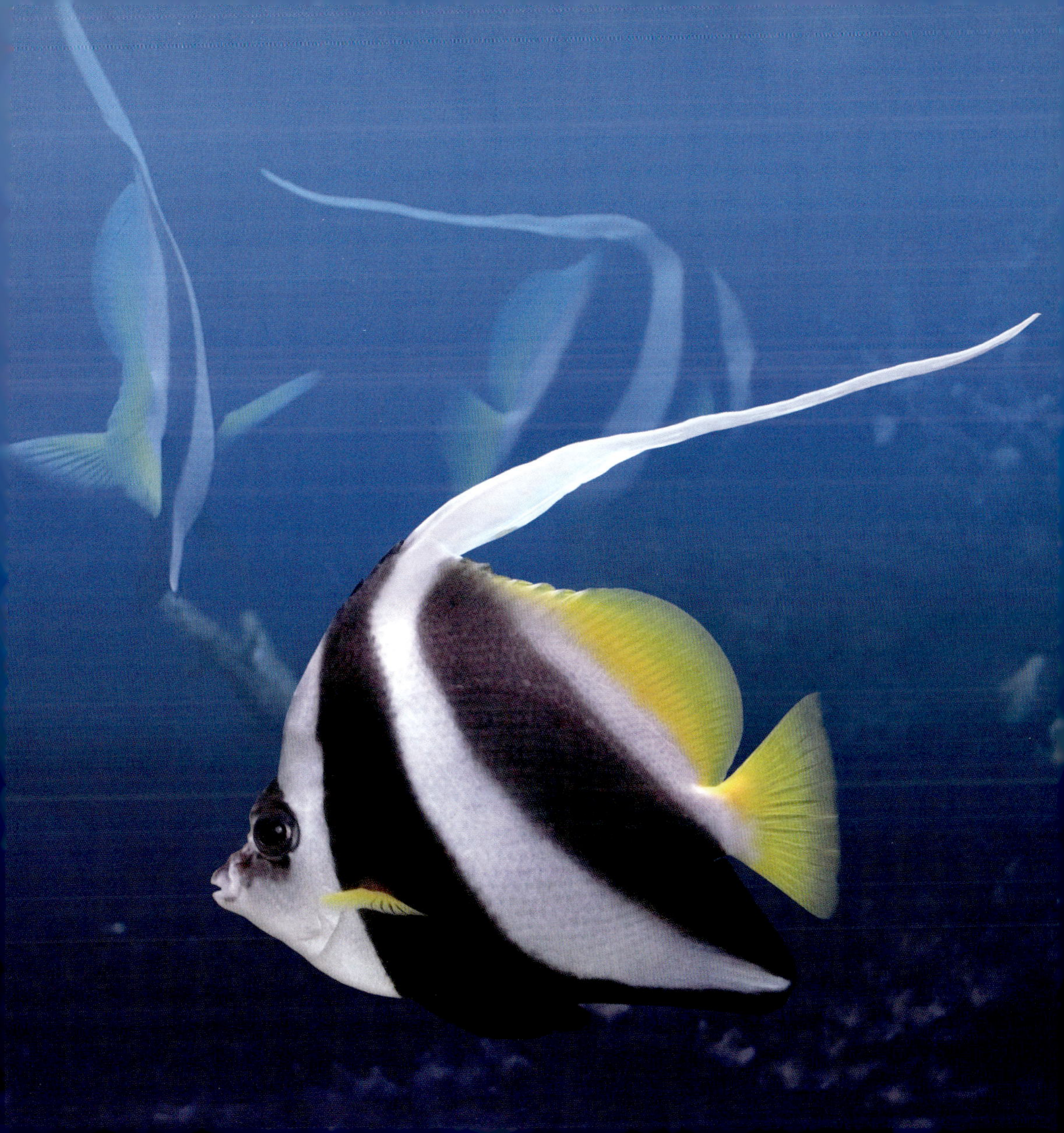

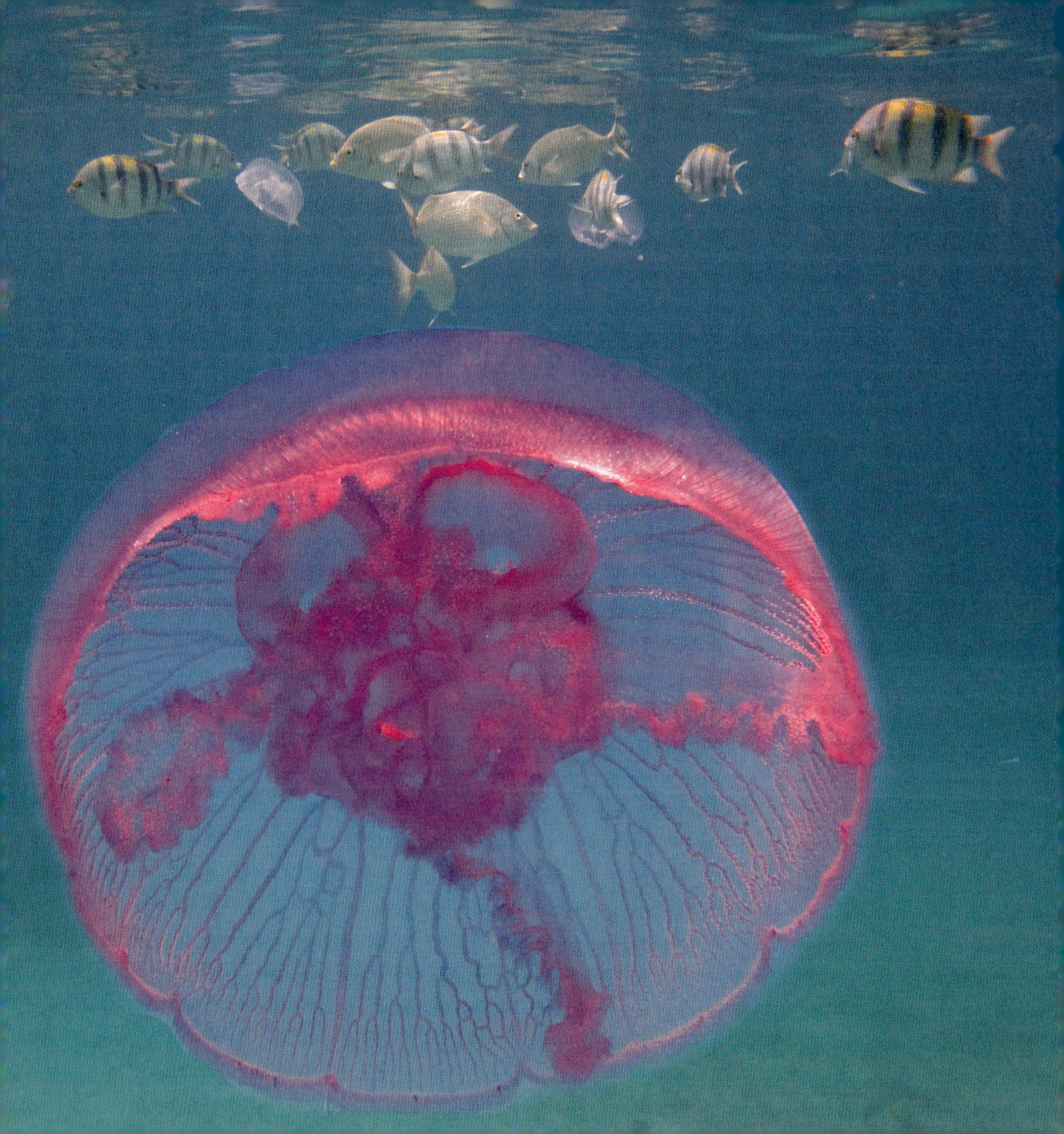

Transparent natures

are often deceptive in their depth;

these pebbles at the bottom of the fountain

are further from us than we think.

Nathaniel Hawthorne

I must be a mermaid.

I have no fear of depths and a great fear of shallow living.

Anaïs Nin

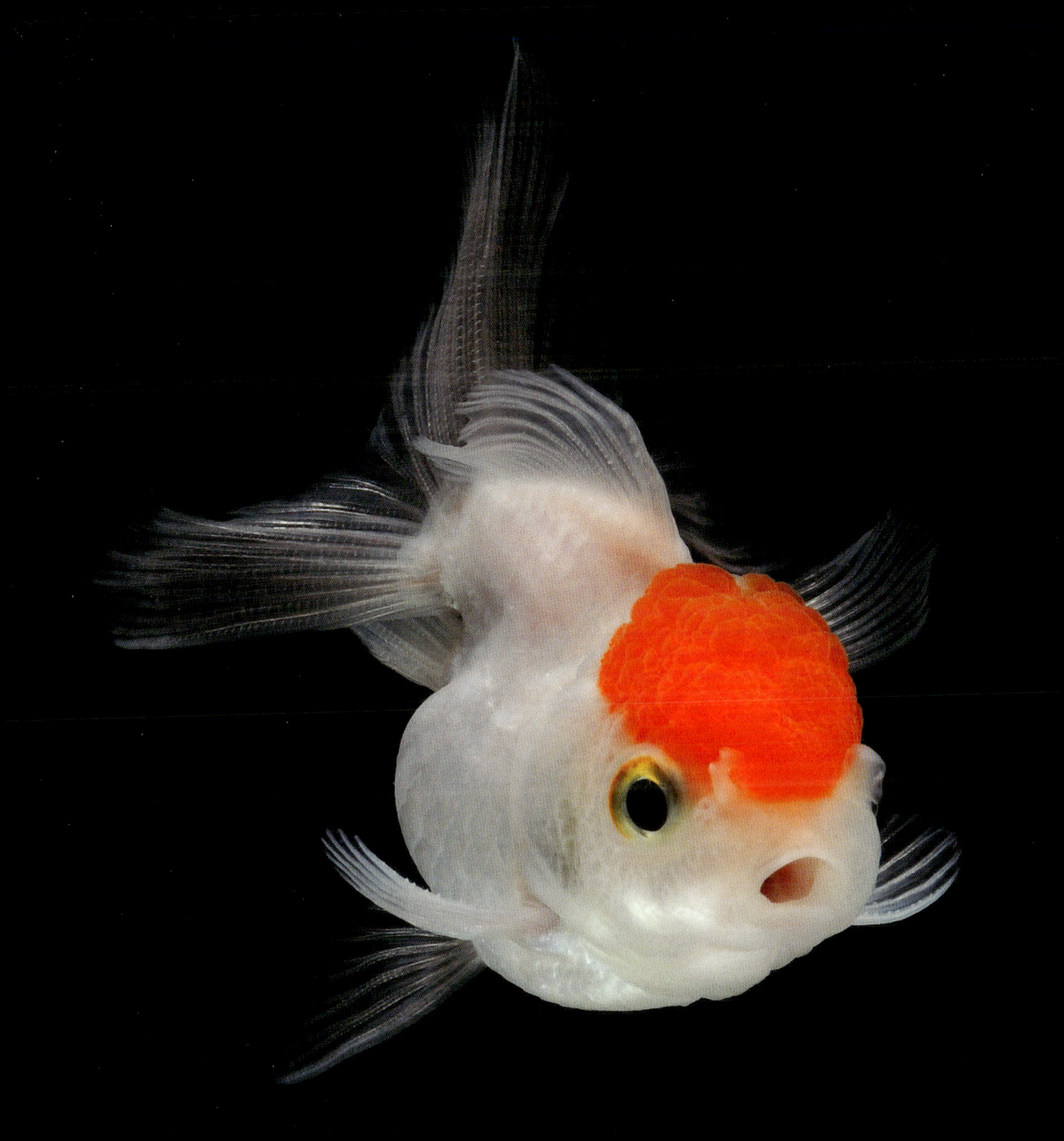

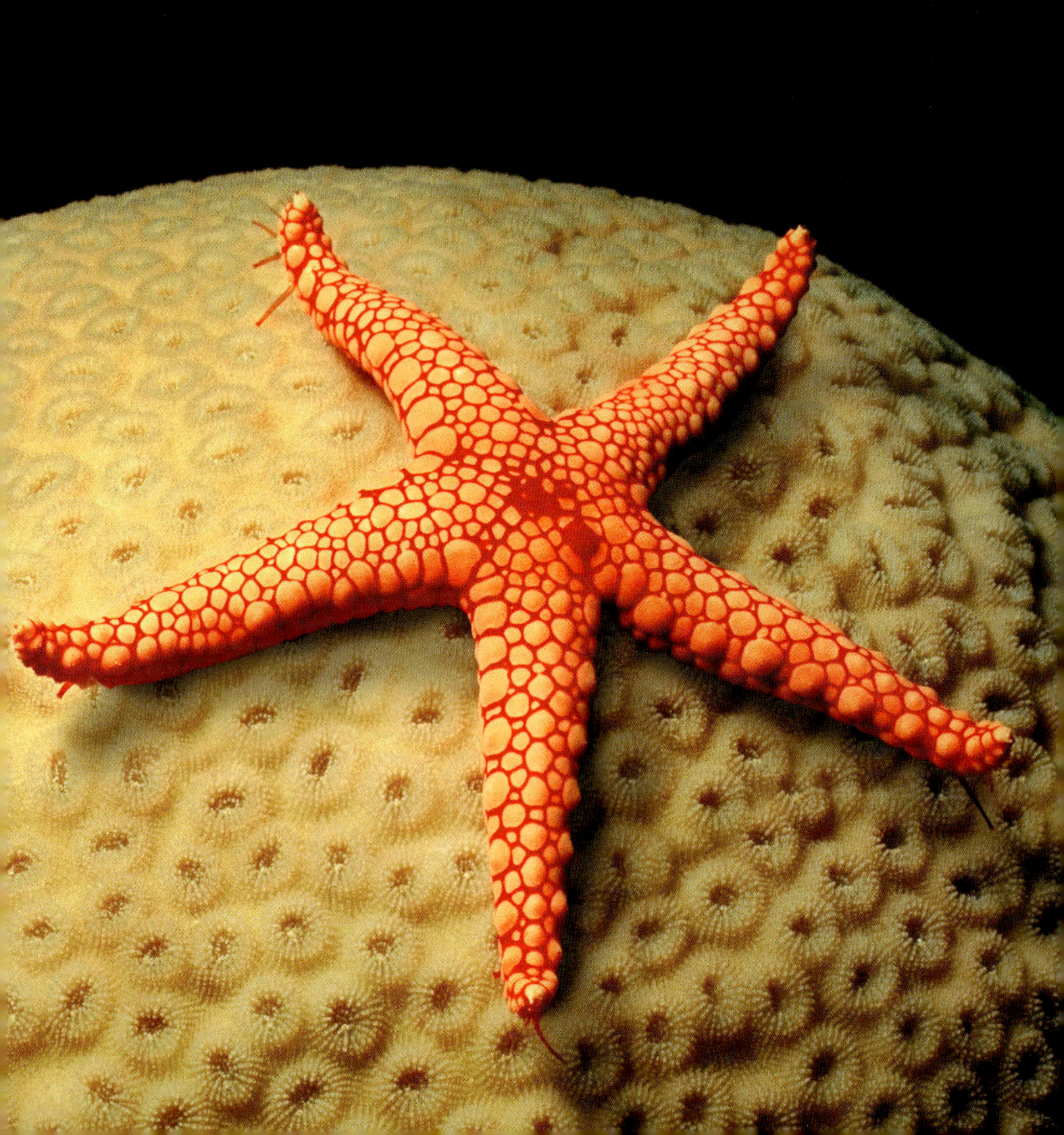

Our life is

what our thoughts make it.

Marcus Aurelius

In the depth of the sea

        the water is still;

the heaviest grief

        is borne in silence;

the deepest love

        flows through

        the eyes and touch;

the purest joy

        is unspeakable.

T. T. Lynch

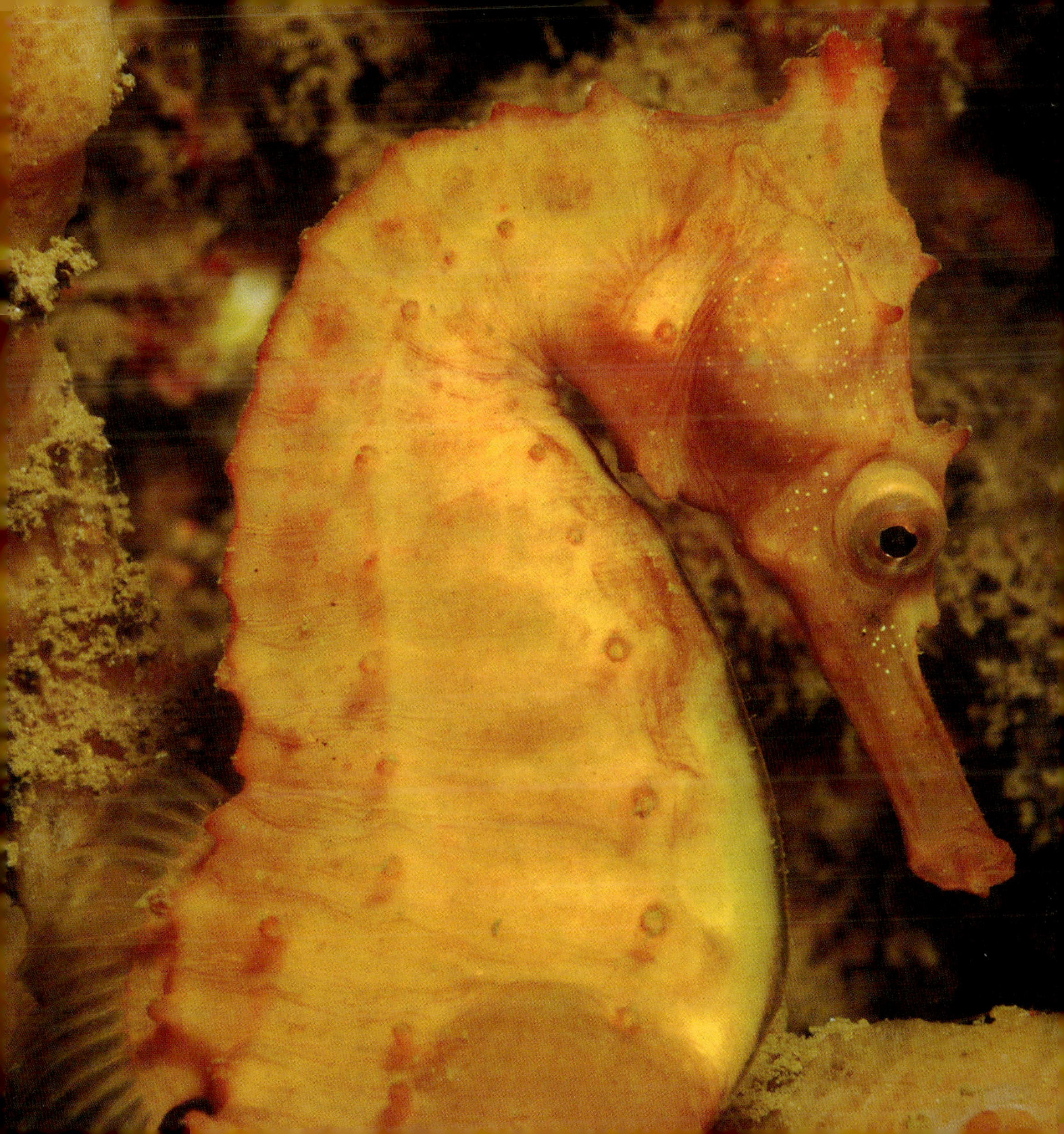

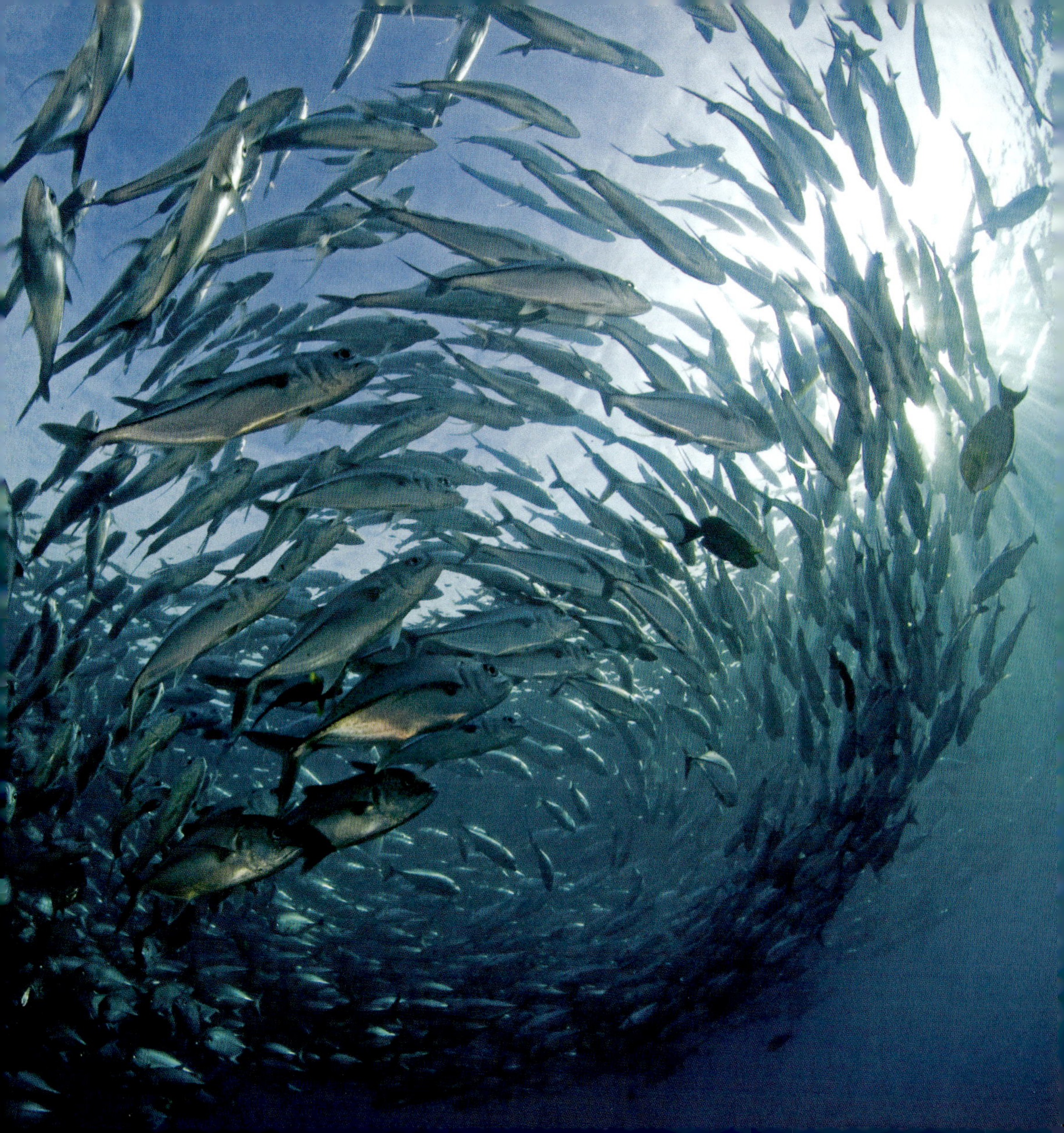

The populace is like the sea
motionless in itself,
but stirred by every wind,
even the lightest breeze.

Titus Livius

There's
nothing funnier
than the
human animal.

Walt Disney

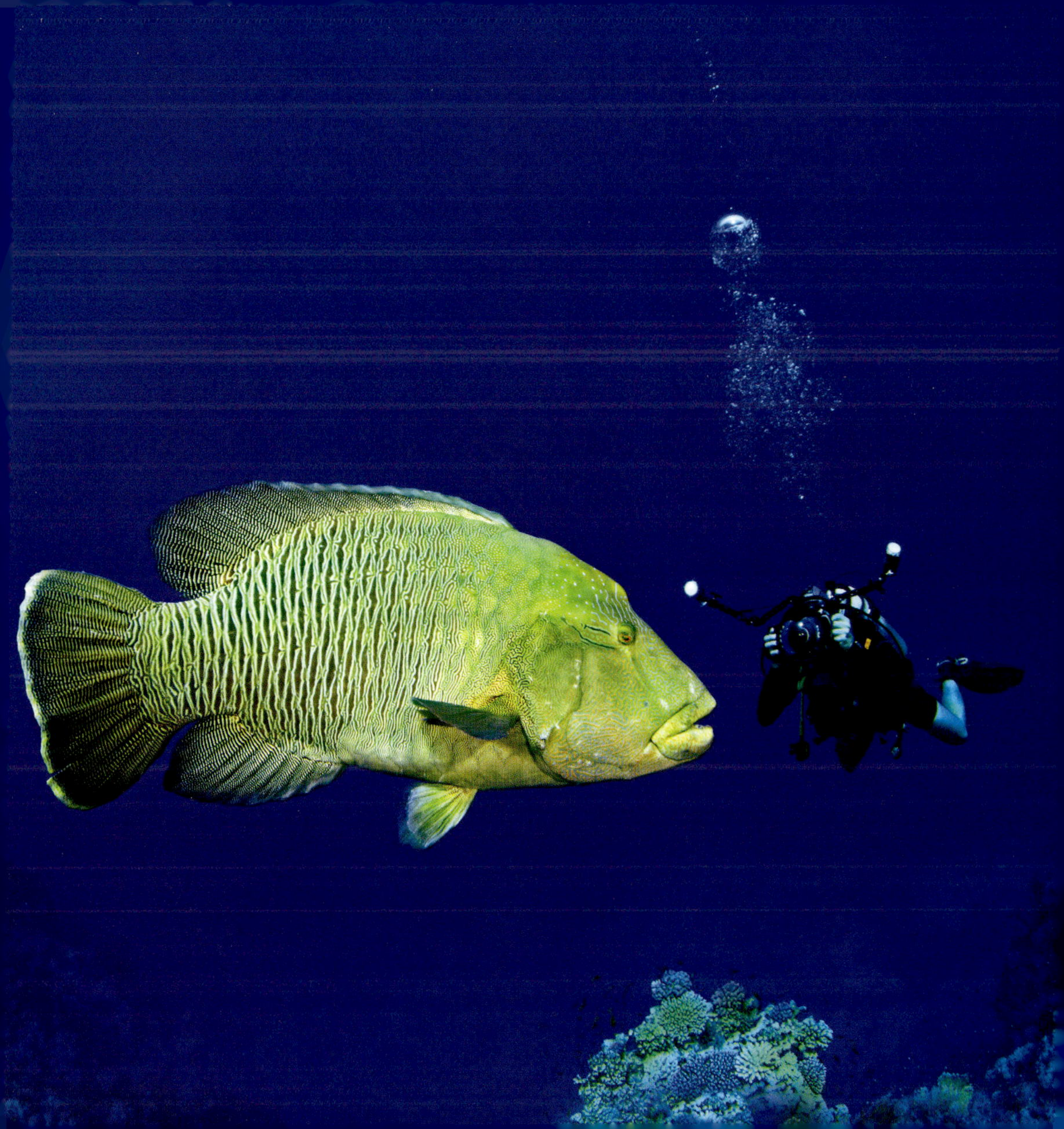

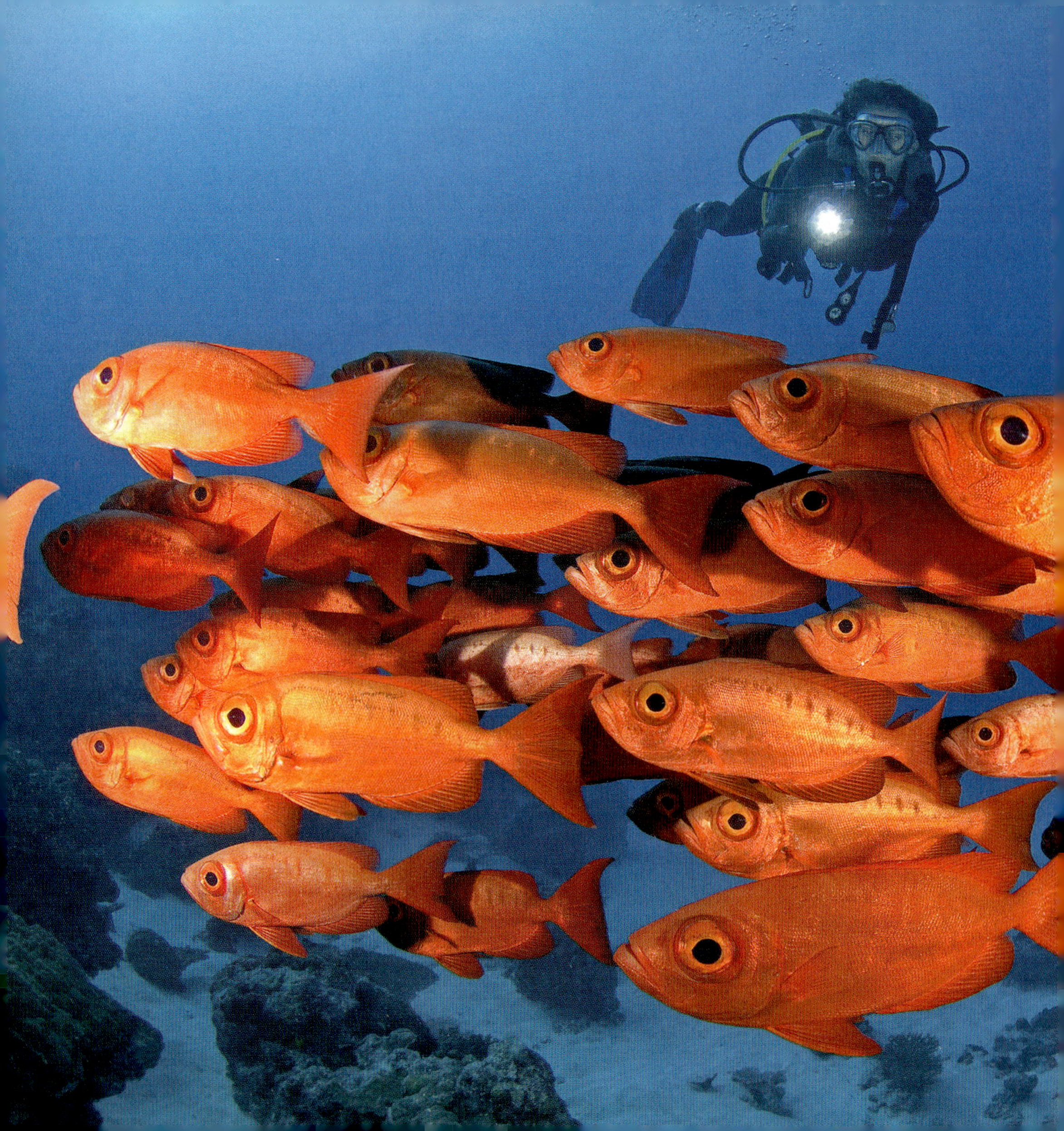

All men are equal before fish.

Herbert Hoover

Don't tell fish stories
where the people know you;
but particularly,
don't tell them where
they know the fish.

Mark Twain

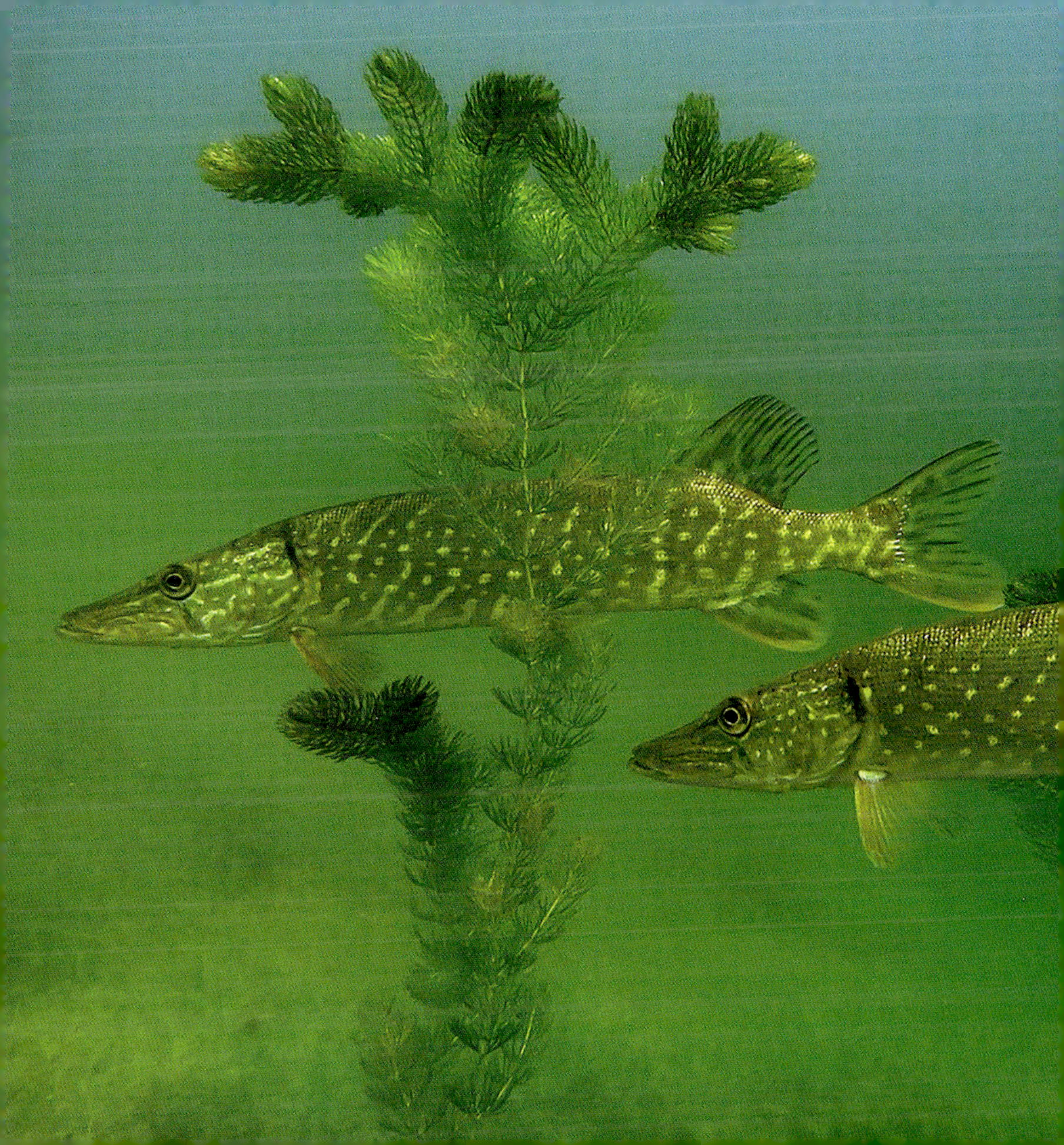

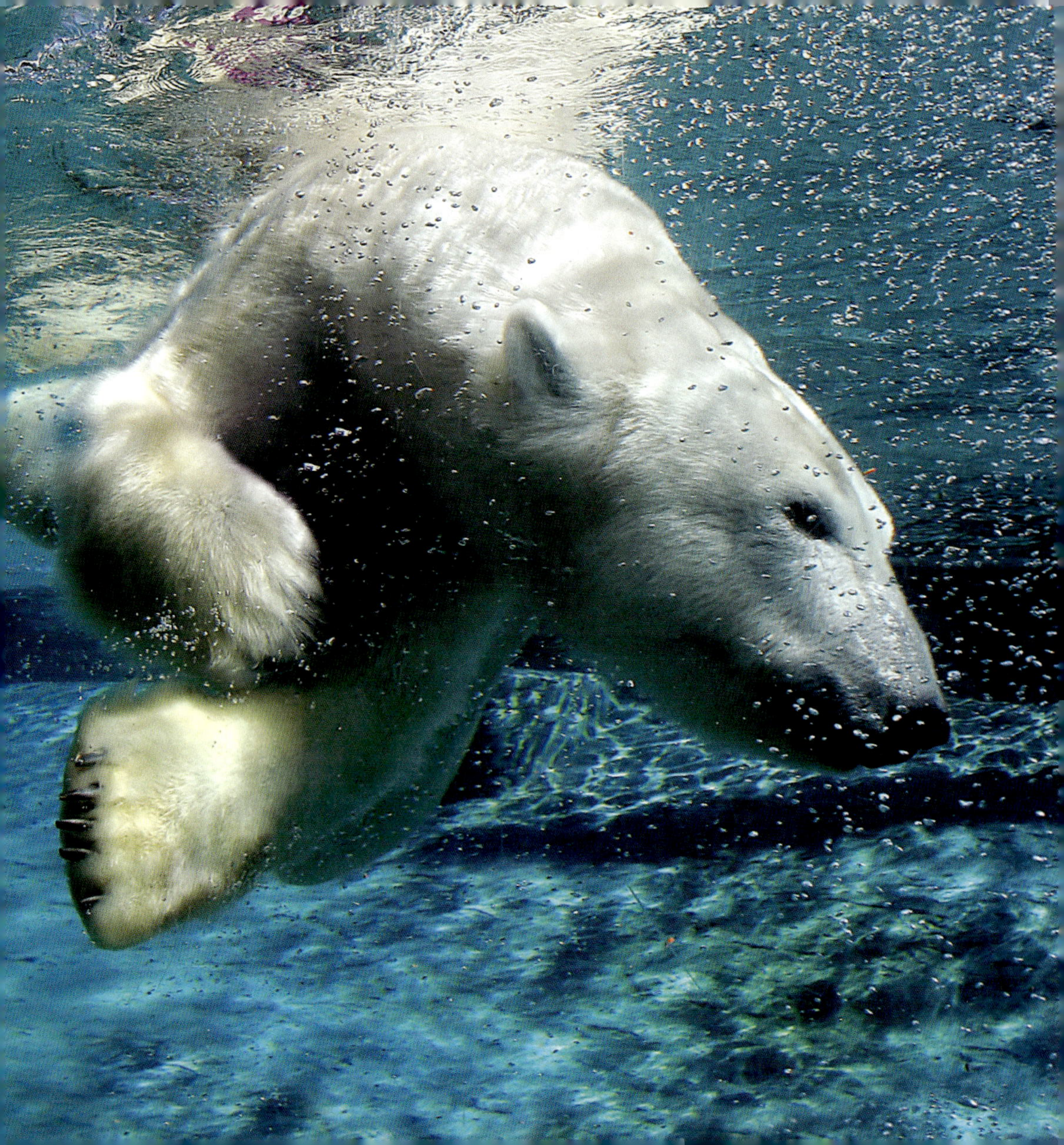

Chance

is always powerful.

Let your hook

always be cast;

in the pool where you

least expect it,

there will be fish.

Ovid

The water in a vessel
is sparkling;
the water in the sea
is dark.
The small truth
has words
which are clear;
the great truth has
great silence.

Rabindranath Tagore

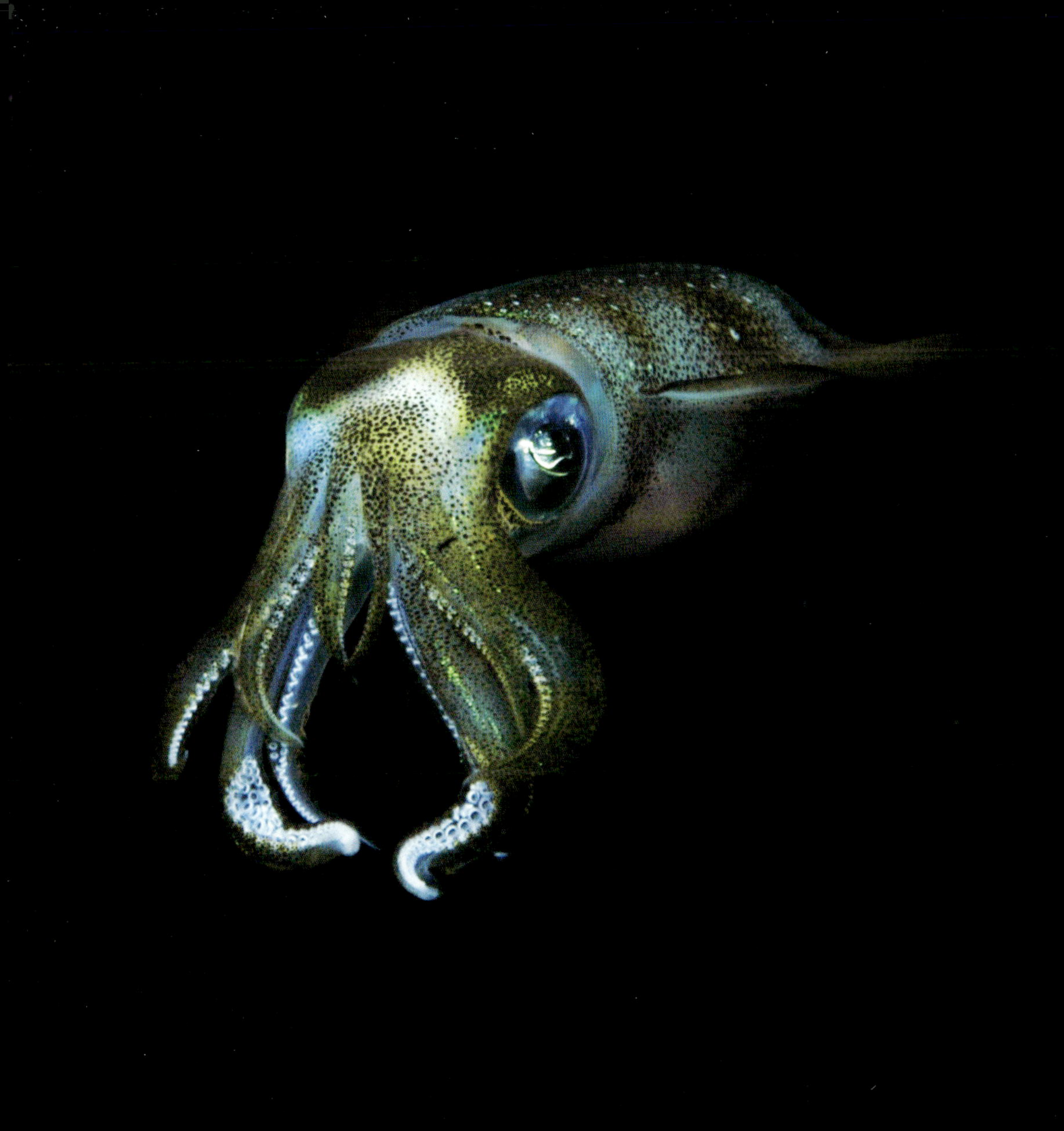

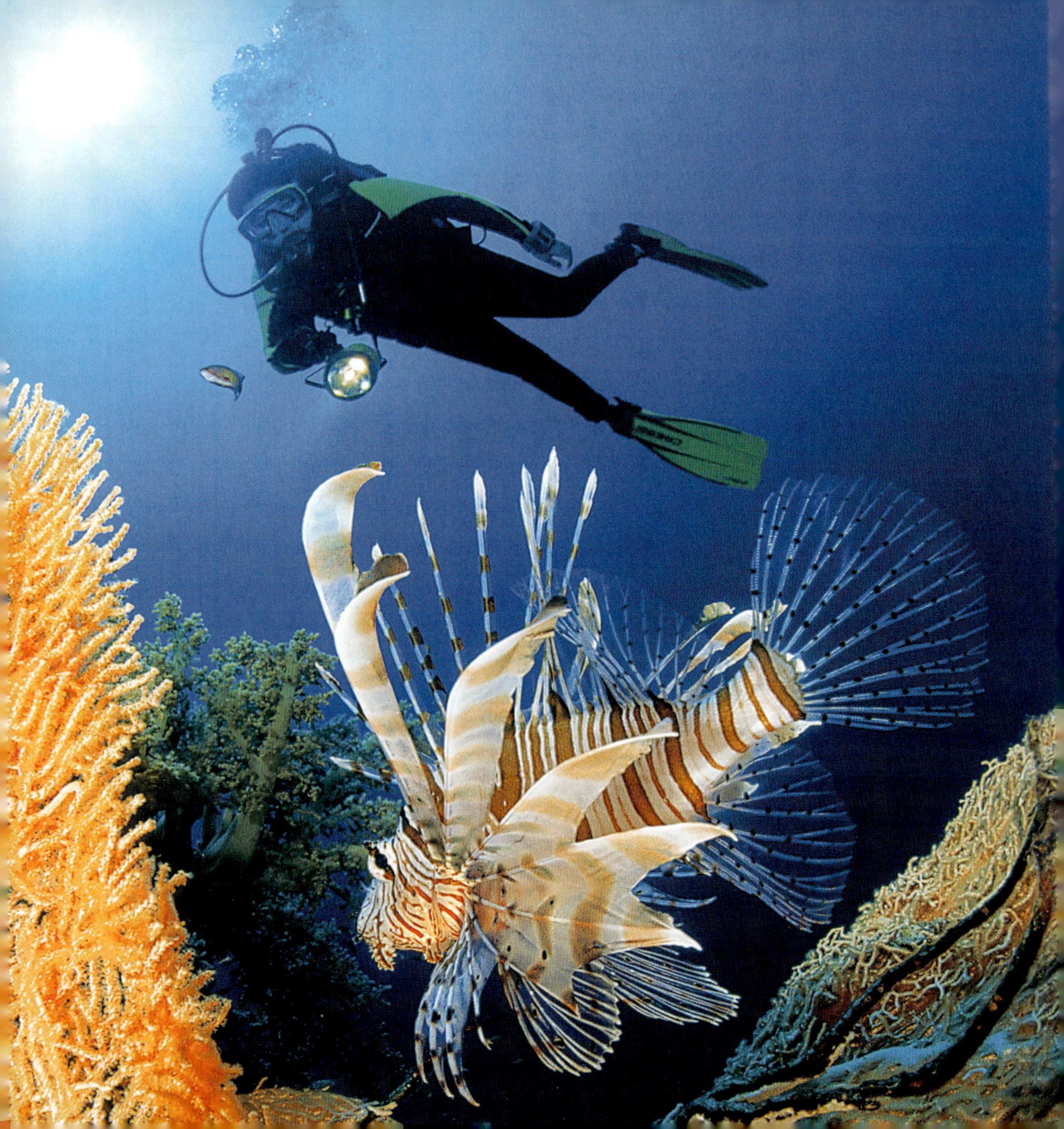

Let [love] rather be a moving sea between the shores of your souls.

Khalil Gibran

Pure water is the world's first and foremost medicine.

Slovakian Proverb

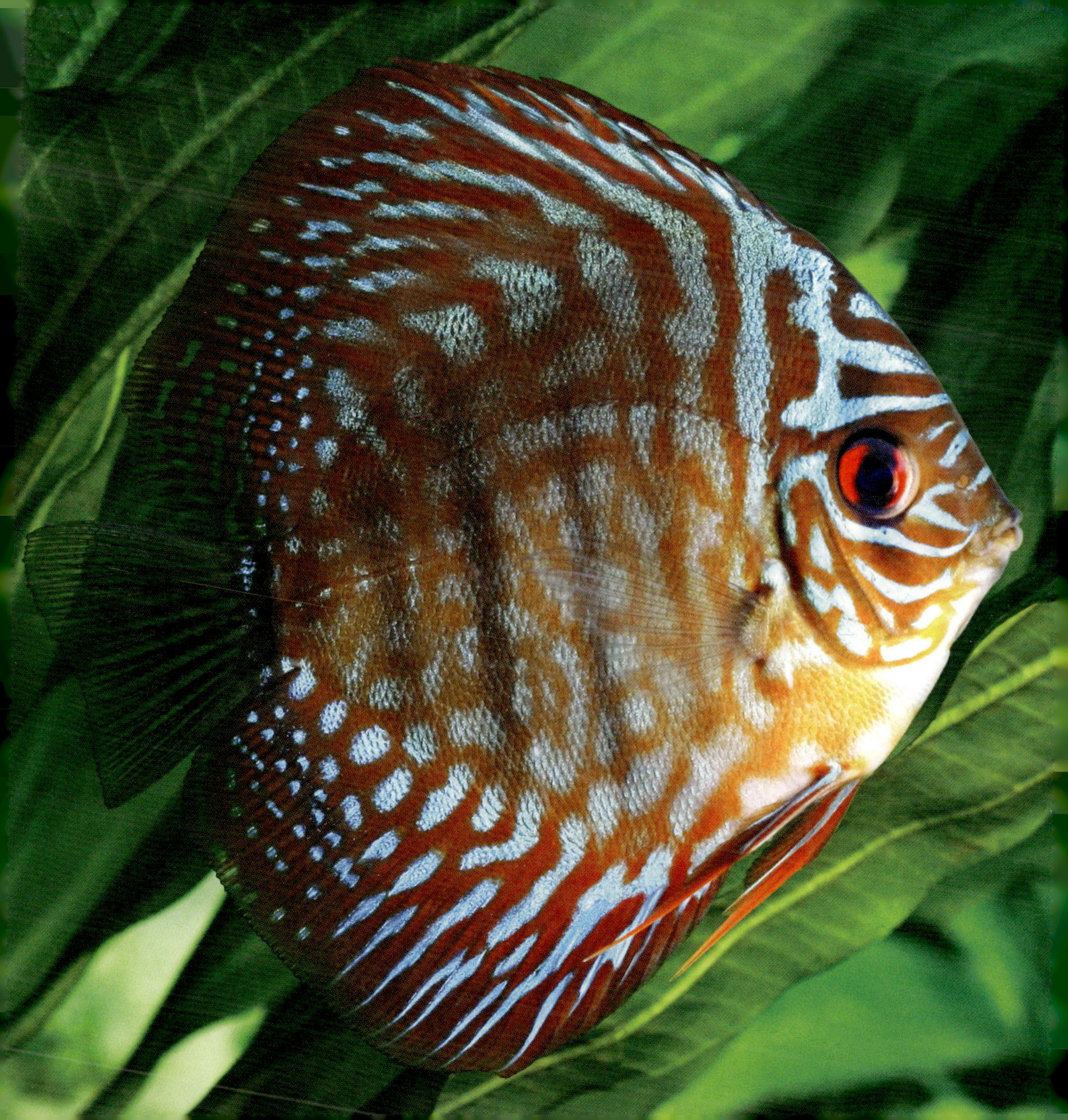

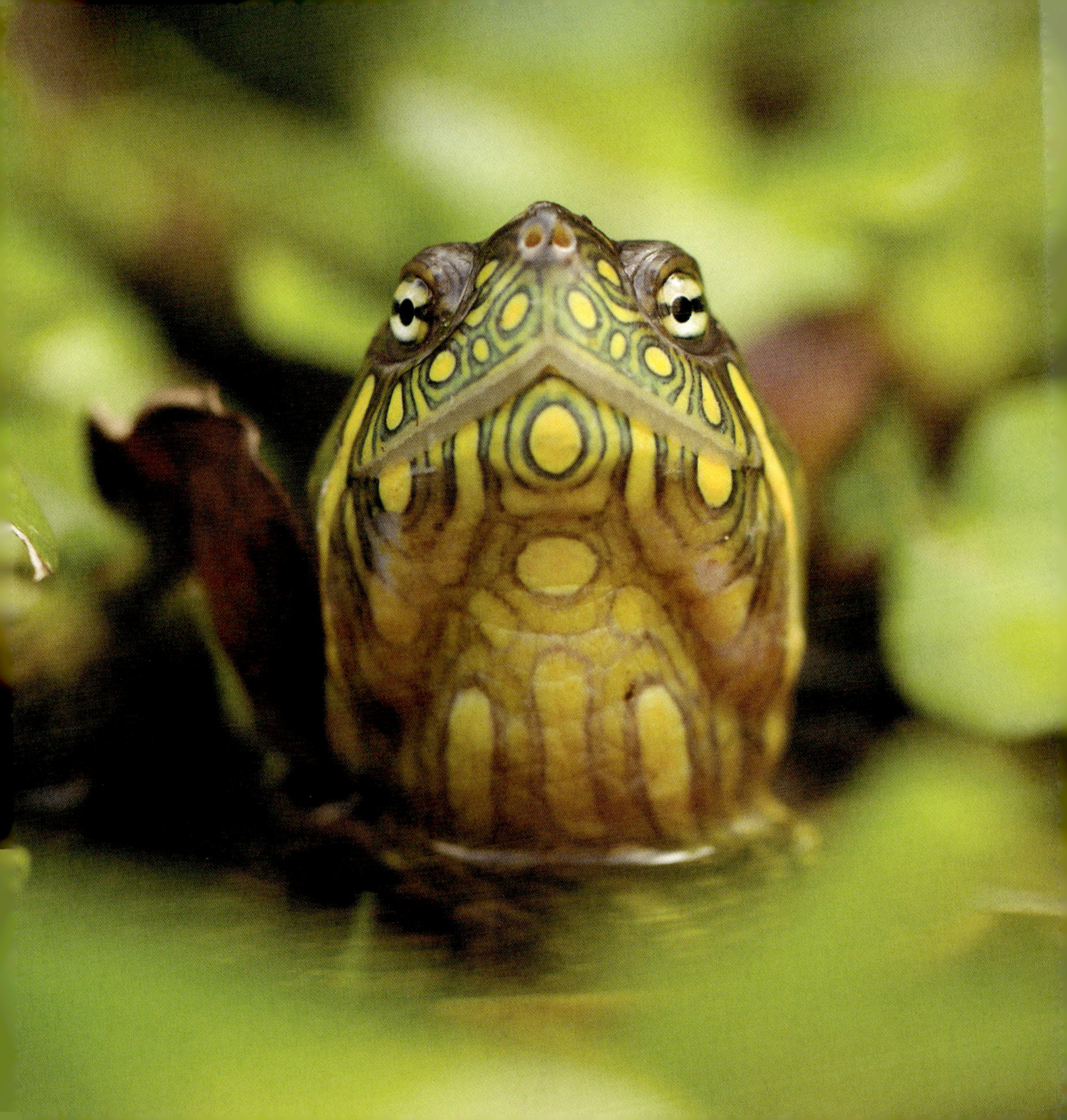

Green is the prime color

of the world,

and that from which

its loveliness arises.

Pedro Calderon de la Barca

There are two ways to live:
you can live as if
nothing is a miracle;
you can live as if
everything is a miracle.

Albert Einstein

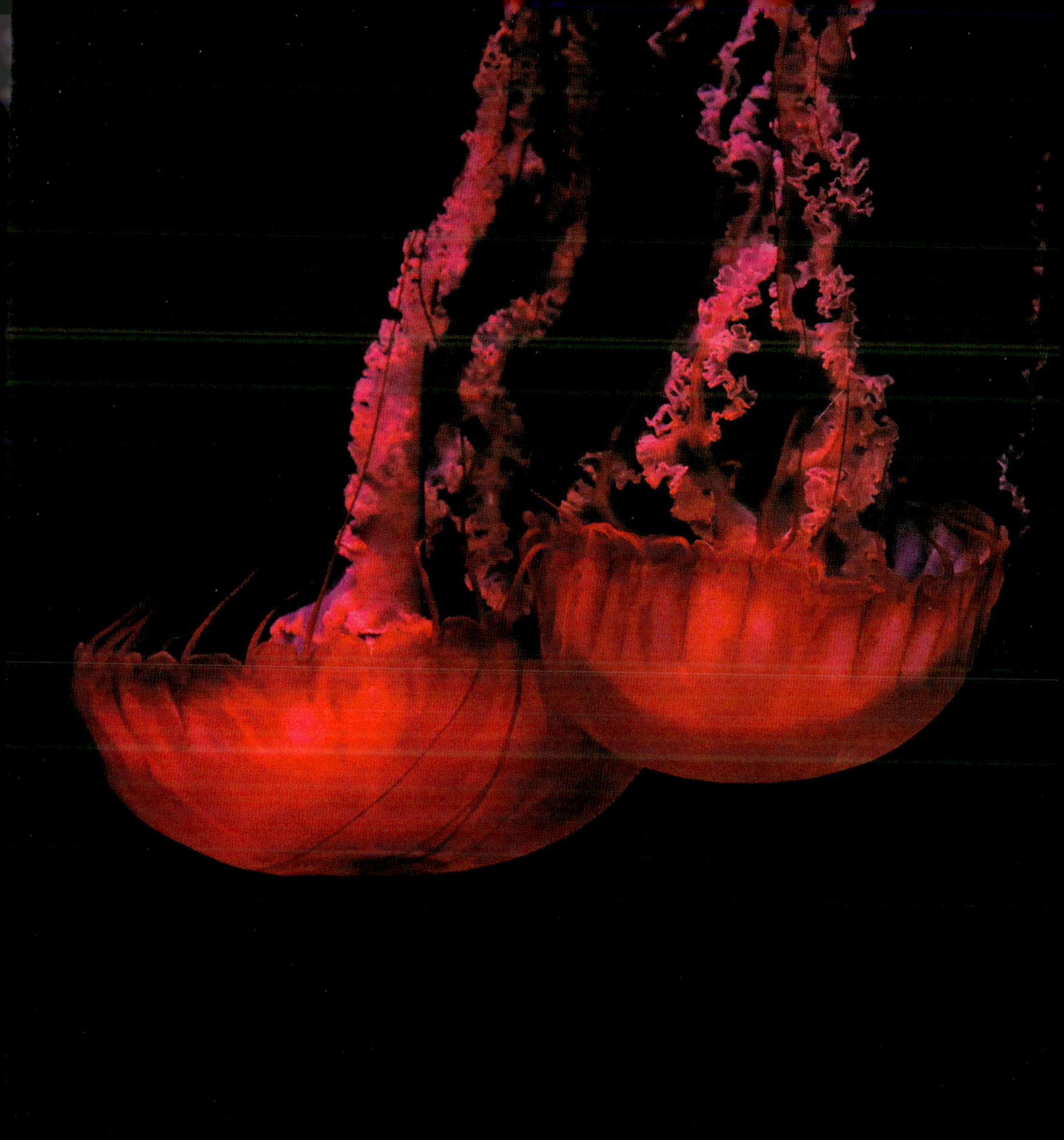

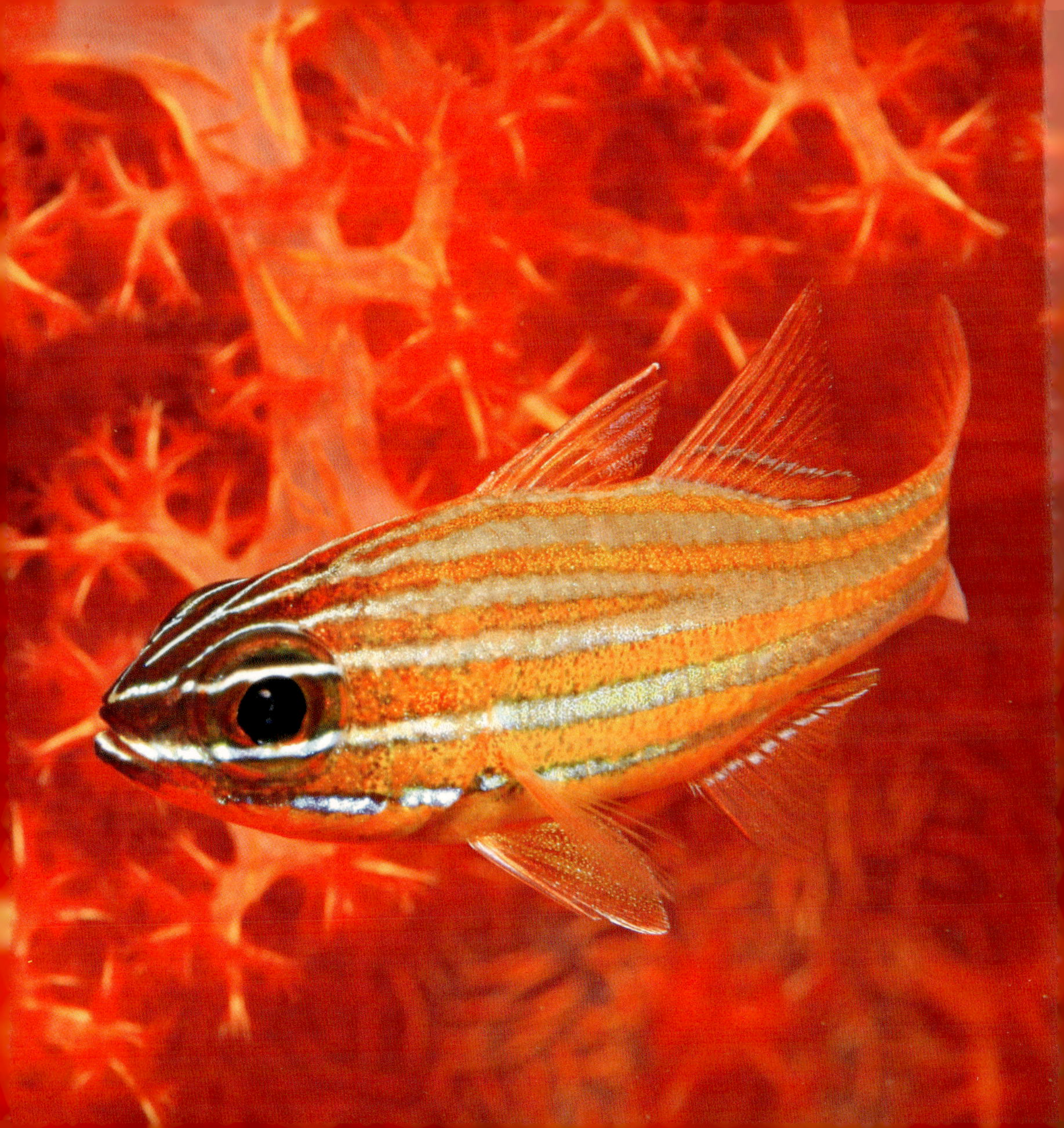

Those who find beauty
in all of nature
will find themselves
at one with the secrets
of life itself.

Louis Wolfe Gilbert

The sea, once it casts its spell,

holds one in its net of wonder forever.

Jacques Yves Cousteau

Quotes *for* Life®